The Essential
Sous vide
Cookbook

Sarah Orwell

Copyright © 2018 by Sarah Orwell
All Rights Reserved

No part of this publication may be reproduced, stored in a retrieval system, or transmitted in any form or by any means, electronic, mechanical, photocopying, recording, scanning or otherwise, except as permitted under Sections 107 or 108 of the 1976 United States Copyright Act, without the prior written permission of the Publisher, except for the inclusion of brief quotations in a review.

Disclaimer and Terms of Use
The Author and Publisher has strived to be as accurate and complete as possible in the creation of this book, notwithstanding the fact that he does not warrant or represent at any time that the contents within are accurate due to the rapidly changing nature of the Internet. While all attempts have been made to verify information provided in this publication, the Author and Publisher assumes no responsibility for errors, omissions, or contrary interpretation of the subject matter herein. Any perceived slights of specific persons, peoples, or organizations are unintentional. In practical advice books, like anything else in life, there are no guarantees of results. Readers are cautioned to rely on their own judgment about their individual circumstances and act accordingly. This book is not intended for use as a source of legal, medical, business, accounting or financial advice. All readers are advised to seek services of competent professionals in the legal, medical, business, accounting, and finance fields.

- **7 Delicious and Mouth-watering Recipes**
- **Never Sacrifice Flavors for Good Health**

Claim Your FREE Recipes Here
http://inspiyration.com/7dhd

Contents

- Introduction 8
  - How Does Cooking Sous Vide Work? 8
  - Cooking Temperatures 9
  - Getting to Understand Sous Vide Machines 10
    - Sous Vide Ovens: 10
    - Immersion Circulator: 11
    - Choose the DIY Method Instead: 12
  - Essential Cooking Equipment: 13
    - Vacuum Sealer: 14
    - Plastic Bags: 14
    - Mason Jars: 15
    - Immersion Circulator: 15
    - Water Basin: 15
    - Nonstick Pan and Cast-iron Skillet: 15
    - Saucepan: 16
  - Benefits of Sous Vide Cooking 16
  - The Safety of Cooking Sous Vide: 17
- Chapter 1: Sous Vide Fish & Seafood Recipes 18
  - Sous Vide Lobster 18
  - Teriyaki Salmon 20
  - Whole Red Snapper 22
  - Salmon with Yogurt Dill Sauce 24
  - Crusted Tuna Fish 26
  - Sole Fish & Bacon 28
  - Coriander Garlic Squids 30
  - Swordfish Piccata 32
  - Lazy Man's Lobster 34
- Chapter 2: Sous Vide Lamb & Beef Recipes 36
  - Spiced Beef Brisket 36
  - Simple Spiced Ribs 38
  - Beef Stroganoff 40
  - Cumin-Spiced Lamb Chops 42
  - Sous Vide Burgers 44

- Sicilian Lamb Shanks 46
- Sunday Roast 48
- Beef Wellington 50
- Short Ribs Provençale 52
- Rolled Beef 54

Chapter 3: Sous Vide Summer Recipes 56
- Crab Zucchini Roulade & Mousse 56
- Mexican Street Corn 58
- Yukon Gold Potato Salad 60
- Radish Feta Salad 62
- Aromatic Chicken 63
- Mediterranean Chicken 65
- Garlic Parmesan Broccolini 67
- Turkey Burgers 68
- Chicken Thighs & Herbed Rice 70
- Carnitas Tacos 72

Chapter 4: Sous Vide Autumn/Fall Recipes 74
- Curried Acorn Squash 74
- Bacon Brussels Sprouts 75
- Indian Style Pork 77
- Whiskey Infused Apples 79
- Sous Vide Garlic Confit 80
- Sweet Potato Salad 81
- Chicken Marsala 83
- Warm Assorted Broccoli Salad 85
- Pumpkin Puree 89
- Sous Vide Cauliflower Puree 91

Chapter 5: Sous Vide Spring Recipes 93
- Asparagus with Hollandaise 93
- French Herb Omelet 94
- Corn on The Cob 96
- Spicy Ginger Tofu 97
- Sous Vide Artichokes 99
- Cauliflower Soup 101
- Butter-Poached Asparagus with Fresh Mint 103
- Green Sesame Salad 104

    Cauliflower Alfredo 106

    Sous Vide Glazed Turnips 108

Chapter 6: Sous Vide Winter Recipes 109

    Brussels Sprouts Sous Vide 109

    Caramelized Leek & Salmon Egg Muffins 110

    Buttercup Squash Cordial 112

    Delicata Squash Puree 113

    Leek Salad 114

    Sweet Potato Soup 116

    Miso-Butter Japanese Turnips 118

    Pickled Fennel Salad 119

    Rosemary & Lemon-Infused Salmon 121

Chapter 7: Sous Vide Poultry Recipes 123

    Chicken Wings 123

    Fried Chicken 125

    Sticky Duck Wings 127

    Sage Infused Turkey 129

    Chicken Cordon Bleu 130

    Duck a la Orange 132

    Sweet Chicken Teriyaki 134

    Fresh Chicken Salad 136

    Viet-Style Chicken Skewers 138

    Curry Chicken Soup 140

Chapter 8: Sous Vide Pork Recipes 142

    Pulled Pork 142

    Breakfast Sausage Patties 144

    Tokyo-Style Pork Ramen 146

    Pork Knuckles 148

    Pork Medallions 150

    Barbecue Ribs 152

    BLT 153

    Pork Osso Bucco 155

    Spiced Pork Loin Steaks 157

    Honey Mustard Pork Shoulder 159

Chapter 9: Sous Vide Marinades & Sauces Recipes 160

    Béarnaise Sauce 160

    Hollandaise Sauce... 161
    Tomato Sauce.. 162
    Cranberry Sauce.. 164
    Hot Sauce... 165
    Applesauce.. 166
    Sweet and Sour Sauce.. 167
    Basil Tomato Sauce... 169
    Creme Anglaise... 171
    Soy Chili Sauce... 172
    Cherry Sauce... 173

Chapter 10: Sous Vide Cocktail & Dessert Recipes 174
    Orange-Anise Bitters... 174
    Lime-Ginger Gin Tonic 175
    Mocha Coffee Liqueur... 177
    Strawberry Ice Cream.. 178
    Peach Infused Bourbon.. 180
    "Barrel-Aged" Negroni 181
    Tom Collins Cocktail.. 182
    Cherry Manhattan.. 183
    Rummy Eggnog.. 184
    Watermelon Mint Vodka Infusion 186
    Bloody Mary Cocktail.. 187

Conclusion... 189
Index... 190

Introduction

How Does Cooking Sous Vide Work?

For one, it's not as difficult as you think; it's just important that you have the necessary equipment. For Sous Vide recipes, simple ingredients are just fine. As a matter of fact, most recipes only require basic spices to pull them off.

To begin, have your Sous Vide Cooker filled with water and preheated to the temperature of your choice. You can use the heating time for preparation of ingredients. Season ingredients to your liking and have them placed into individual Sous Vide bags. It is important that you use these bags, which are designed for preparing Sous Vide meals, as others bags may cause leakage and destruction of elements.

Once components are in their respective bags, use a vacuum sealer to rid the pack of air. In the absence of a vacuum sealer, you can use the water bath method to vacuum. Using this method, carefully rest the filled bag into a water bath, while preventing water from entering the container. Allow the water's pressure to press the air through the bag's opening. When most, if not all, of the air has been released, have the bag sealed above the water line. After completing these steps, you can finally begin cooking.

When cooking with Sous Vide, mastering temperature and measurements is key. Your handle on these factors will determine your dish's flavor and texture. The range of temperatures for Sous Vide cooking is from 115 to 190F, maintaining a below-boiling temperature. It is key to be constant in temperature during baking. The raising or lowering to single degree can alter a dish's taste and appearance.

Cooking Temperatures

Below is a guide to cooking temperatures:

Food Type	Temperature
White Poultry Meat	140-146F, and up to, but not exceeding 160F
Dark Poultry Meat	176F
Meat	134F, 140F and 150F for rare, medium, and medium well, respectively
Fish	126F and up to, but not exceeding 140F
Eggs	147F (soft boil), 167 (hard boil)
Shellfish	135-140F
Vegetables	185F
Cakes	190F

Getting to Understand Sous Vide Machines

The good news is that they are easy to use; you don't have to be a chef to effectively use them. Two types of Sous Vide methods exist: sous vide ovens (cookers) and immersion circulators. For now, we'll only use the sous vide ovens. These ovens are all-inclusive when it comes to cooking Sous Vide. Each contains a water reservoir (for your vacuum-sealed food), timers (for cooking at accurate temperatures), and digital thermometers.

A few most-recommended machines are:

Sous Vide Ovens:

The simplest way to start a Sous Vide lifestyle is to purchase an all-inclusive sous vide oven. Each includes a reservoir that is precise in heating and maintains the circulation of the water bath. They also include timers for precision, digital thermometers, and sometimes, vacuum sealers for food packaging after a bath.

Many of the Sous Vide ovens, such as the Tribest Sousvant and the Oliso Pro (two of my favorites), are designed to add to the edgy finish and modern appeal of your kitchen. With the Oliso Pro comes an induction cooktop for searing sous vide foods to a finish of a golden-brown floor, without the need of a single pan. Although the less expensive sous vide printers look much like office printers, they can also be used to carry out the same function. Within this price range, I would recommend the Sous Vide Supreme Demi, which is squared, but compact, and is ideal for the smaller-sized family.

Immersion Circulator:

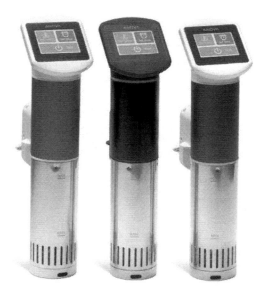

If you like the efficiency and precision of the sous vide oven, but prefer a slightly lower price point, you may need to look into immersion circulators. They are miniature-sized handheld devices, which transform any basin, filled with water, into a sous vide machine.

They pull up water from the basin, heat it to a specific temperature, and empty the water into the same basin. While doing so, the device ensures that the heat and speed of circulation is carefully regulated. A circulator resembles an immersion blender, in terms of shape and size. Therefore, a circulator would take up about the same amount of space as an immersion blender in your kitchen.

The competition, of late, within the market of immersion calculators is unbelievable, as each company seeks to win the most customers. While each holds its own, some are admittedly more sophisticated than others. The Sanshire, a brand that we would recommend, has attractively designed devices with more heating specificity.

Impressively, it can heat water within one-tenth of a single degree (Fahrenheit). Cooks who are more technologically inclined may prefer the Anova WiFi Precision Cooker. Through this device, you can receive phone notifications, regarding the status of a dish you're cooking. After choosing a circulator, you can either buy a sous vide container or use a large pot you already own for a water basin. The only thing left for you to buy is a vacuum sealer before you can actually start cooking.

Choose the DIY Method Instead:

Perhaps, you're thinking, "Why invest in a brand-new kitchen appliance just to experiment with a new cooking style?" That's fine; we've figured out DIY options just for you. To vacuum seal your food, a vacuum sealer would be great, but if you don't have one at home, you can make one yourself. All you need is a large bowl with water, and a Ziploc freezer bag.

Place the food into the Ziploc bag, and lower the bag into the water, permitting the escape of air from the top of the bag. When the bag is lowered into the water almost to the zipper point, seal the bag. You would have just used a technique referred to in this book as the "water method" seal.

This method is useful, whether using a DIY vacuum sealer or a ready-made one and is especially helpful when using recipes that require liquid being placed into a bag. It can get a little ugly, using an electric vacuum sealer. Secondly, you need a pot that regulates low temperatures. Here is where your crock pot or rice cooker comes in handy. Using its "keep warm" button and a thermometer, you can monitor the temperature to which the button reaches. The temperature is used to calculate the different cooking times for the recipes below.

It's possible that, after getting used to your homemade sealer, you develop the desire to get a professional sous vide appliance. Whether you choose Oliso Pro or to keep using your homemade sealer, it's certain that your sous vide meals will impress family and friends!

Essential Cooking Equipment:

We mentioned the different types of Sous Vide appliances and machines last chapter, as well as their respective benefits. Now we'll further discuss the components needed to run a Sous Vide kitchen.

Vacuum Sealer:

Because most machines don't include a vacuum sealer, even if you have an "all-inclusive" appliance, you'll need to purchase a sealer. If you want to save on cash, you can use the DIY method mentioned earlier, but purchasing one would only cost you $15 or less.

Plastic Bags:

Usually, your purchased vacuum sealer would include a roll of plastic bags (heavy duty), designed specifically for the machine. If you are following recipes that include the water seal method (DIY alternative), you'll need to have some freezer bags on hand. Refrain from using sandwich bags instead of the recommended freezer bags, as sandwich bags are not as sturdy as freezer bags. Using freezer bags would mean that a bag's contents wouldn't degrade in water because of the tougher seal that it possesses.

Mason Jars:

There are recipes within this book that utilize mason jars instead of plastic bags, especially when cooking dishes such as custards or cakes. Custards and cakes, as well as many other dishes, are cooked with a particular form or shape. Ensure that the lids of jars are always screwed on tight. You can use a method, referred to as the "finger tight" method, with which many canners are familiar. Using this method, cracks are prevented by the allowance of steam's escape.

Immersion Circulator:

As explained in the last chapter, immersion circulators warm the water and disperse heat evenly within the basin. If you purchase a Sous Vide oven, you won't need one, since it has a built-in circulator.

Water Basin:

The thing you'll find most convenient about the immersion circulator is that it is operable with any of the pots you have at home. However, to obtain the most precise results, you'd want to buy a container (preferably plastic, a better insulator than metal) specifically for cooking sous vide meals. I would recommend using a Cambro container, which is a favorite among restaurants, found in several sizes. For the purpose of cooking for an entire family, it would be best to use the 4.75-gallon version. (A separate basin is not needed if you already have a sous vide oven.)

Nonstick Pan and Cast-iron Skillet:

If you want the appearance of your meal to be of restaurant caliber, you can fire it up in a pan after it is removed from the sous vide. You can use a decent nonstick skillet to do the trick, but for best results, use a hot cast iron or a copper skillet.

Saucepan:

There are a few recipes within this book that require additional steps for making a sauce. It is important that you have a saucepan ready for use when following these particular recipes.

Benefits of Sous Vide Cooking

Many wonder if Sous Vide cooking is even worth all the fuss it gets. If you ever find yourself wondering why you should try it, simply consider one of the following benefits.

1. Tenderness

Tenderness of food is one of the main advantages sous vide has over traditional cooking. Because the food never gets hotter than the water it is in a low temperature is always sustained throughout the process. Tenderness is retained because the meat cells don't burst during cooking and collagen located in the tissue of the meat is broken down without the protein being heated up so that it loses moisture.

2. Moisture Retention

Moisture retention is another advantage of sous vide because it utilizes air tight bags to keep the food, this container creates a moist environment that preserves features such as aromas and moisture that would normally be lost during traditional cooking methods. This enhances your food because it is now cooked with this added juice, which brings out the foods true flavor and texture.

3. Simplicity

One of the drawbacks that often deter people from using the sous vide method is the thought that the technique is a difficult one when in practicality the process is a simple one. The beginning of the process takes up the most effort as it requires preparation. Sous vide follows a linear process once this is mastered the extra time and effort that is exerted in traditional cooking is not needed.

The Safety of Cooking Sous Vide:

As with the introduction to all new concepts, there is skepticism regarding its legitimacy and safety. Some people question the cooking of foods in plastic bags, while others raise eyebrows about cooking at low temperatures.

While cooking in plastic does sound like a bad idea, and there have been concerning reports, is fair to consider the other health risks we take when cooking in any kitchen. Yes, polyethylene has been one to avoid, but every day, we use plastic food containers for eating and storage! Have you thought about the cleanliness of your cooking environments? Admittedly, often times, we cook on less-than-clean countertops.

While plastic is not safe, especially after being used repeatedly or at high temperatures, you can still enjoy safe meals by buying plastic bags from certified retailers. However, Sous Vide bags should only be used once, and cooking with the appliance does not require high temperatures. If you have to miss out on great meals, such as well-done meats and vegetables, let it not be simply because of fear. If, you've considered these and you are still concerned, you can always use canning jars instead.

Another source of major skepticism is bacterial infection, particularly, that of Salmonella. Salmonella only thrives within the temperature range of 40-135F, which is the reason for foods being refrigerated (for an hour) before cooking. This is also the reason for our cooking at certain temperatures before all foods are served and eaten.

Therefore, once you are cooking clean foods in a clean environment, ensuring that foods are refrigerated before cooking, you have no reason to be apprehensive. Vacuum-sealing fresh steak or fish, then, at a constant temperature, cooking for longer periods of time prohibits the growth of any bacteria. With the extent to which temperature is controlled precisely, Sous Vide cooking is actually safer than more traditional means. Sous Vide provides precautionary measures for all concerns one may have by using danger-free plastic and lower temperatures for cooking. These measures ensure that you can enjoy Sous Vide meals without the thought of threats to your health and well-being.

Chapter 1: Sous Vide Fish & Seafood Recipes

Sous Vide Lobster

Ingredients
-
- 1lb. lobster tail, cleaned
- ¾ cup butter, cubed
- 2 sprigs tarragon
- 1 lime, cut into wedges
- Salt, to taste

Directions
1. Preheat Sous Vide cooker to 134 degrees F.
2. In a Sous Vide bag, combine lobster tail, cubed butter, tarragon, and salt.
3. Vacuum seal the bag. Submerge the bag in a water bath and cook 1 hour.
4. Remove the bag from the water bath. Open carefully and transfer the lobster onto a plate. Drizzle the lobster tail with cooking/butter sauce.
5. Serve with lime wedges.

Cook's Tip: Lobster cooked at 130 – 135 degrees F produces a more tender lobster than what you get if it was cooked traditionally. It will be meaty. If you prefer a firmer texture, consider raising the temperature to 140 degrees for about 20 minutes.

Serves: 4   **Prep Time: 10mins**   **Cook Time: 1 hr.**
Calories: 412   **Protein: 22.1g**   **Carbs: 2g**   **Fat: 35.5g**

Teriyaki Salmon

Ingredients
-
- 1-inch fresh ginger, peeled and sliced
- 10 oz. skinless salmon fillets
- 4 oz. egg noodles
- 1 tablespoon sesame oil
- ½ cup + 1 teaspoon teriyaki sauce
- 1 tablespoon sesame seeds, toasted
- 2 teaspoons soy sauce
- 2 teaspoons thinly sliced scallions
- 4 oz. lettuce, chopped
- 1/8 small red onion, sliced thinly
- 1 tablespoon roasted sesame dressing

Directions
1. Add a half of your teriyaki sauce evenly to 2 vacuum pack bags with your salmon, seal, and set to marinate in the refrigerator for about 15 minutes.
2. Set the Sous Vide cooker to preheat to 131F.

3. Add your vacuum bags in the bath and allow to cook for about 15 minutes.
4. Cook egg noodles using the directions on the package.
5. Drain well, return to cooking pot and stir in sesame oil and soy sauce, reserving one teaspoon. Divide pasta between serving plates.
6. Combine the other half of teriyaki sauce, ginger, soy sauce, and scallions to a small bowl and stir to combine.
7. Combine onion and lettuce then drizzle with a teaspoon of roasted sesame dressing.
8. When the timer goes off, remove salmon from the water bath, reserving cooking liquid.
9. Top the pasta with salmon fillets and drizzle all with reserved cooking liquid.
10. Garnish salmon with sesame seeds and serve with prepared salad and dipping sauce.

Cook's Tip: The temperature uses in this recipe will get you a well - done serving of salmon. If you prefer a rarer salmon fillet then consider decreasing the temperature to 120 or even 115 degrees F.

Serves: 2   **Prep Time:** 10mins   **Cook Time:** 15mins
Calories: 291   **Protein:** 33g   **Carbs:** 15.2g   **Fat:** 11.2g

Whole Red Snapper

Ingredients
-
- 1 small red snapper, cleaned and gutted
- 1 teaspoon salt
- 1 teaspoon pepper
- 4 garlic cloves, crushed
- 2 sprigs rosemary
- 1 lemon, cut into wedges
- 2 tablespoons butter, cut into cubes
-

Directions
1. Preheat the water bath to 140 degrees F. Season the fish all over with salt and pepper.
2. Stuff the center of the fish with garlic, rosemary, half the lemon, and butter. Seal into a bag and place in water bath.
3. Cook 60 minutes. Serve with remaining lemon wedges.

Cook's Tip: Sous vide Snapper can also be enjoyed with a fluffy serving of rice or even a vibrant Fattoush salad.

Serves: 2 **Prep Time: 20mins** **Cook Time: 1 hr.**
Calories: 800 **Protein: 140.29g** **Carbs: 4.58g** **Fat: 20.77g**

Salmon with Yogurt Dill Sauce

Ingredients
-
- 2 salmon fillets
- ½ teaspoon salt
- ½ teaspoon pepper
- 2-4 sprigs fresh dill

For sauce:
- 1 cup plain Greek yogurt
- 1 tablespoon fresh dill, minced
- Juice of 1 lemon
- ½ teaspoon salt
- ½ teaspoon pepper

Directions
1. Season salmon with salt and pepper.
2. Seal into the bag with dill. Refrigerate ½ hour.

3. Preheat the water bath to 140 degrees F. Place salmon into the water bath and cook 20 minutes. Meanwhile, prepare the sauce. Combine all sauce ingredients and season to taste.
4. When salmon is cooked, arrange on a plate and top with sauce.

Cook's Tip: When cooking multiple servings of salmon in one vacuum bag consider adding a bit of butter to the bag with them to enhance the juices added to your marinade and produces a juicer end product.

Serves: 2   **Prep Time: 10hrs.**   **Cook Time: 20min**
Calories: 498   **Protein: 70.12g**   **Carbs: 10.16g**   **Fat: 18.56g**

Crusted Tuna Fish

Ingredients:
-
- 3 tablespoons all-purpose flour
- 3 tablespoons ground almonds
- ½ tablespoon butter
- 4 5oz. tuna fillets

Marinade:
- 1 pinch chili powder
- 1 pinch salt
- 1 pinch black pepper
- 5 tablespoons vegetable oil
- 2 teaspoons lemon juice

Directions:
1. Preheat Sous Vide cooker to 132 degrees F. Combine the marinade ingredients in a Sous Vide bag.
2. Add the tuna and vacuum seal. Submerge in a water bath and cook 25 minutes.

3. Remove the fish from Sous vide bag. Pat dry the fish. In a bowl, combine all-purpose flour and almonds. Sprinkle with a pinch of salt.
4. Heat the butter in a large skillet. Coat the tuna with the flour-nut mixture and fry in butter until golden brown.
5. Serve warm.

Cook's Tip: Sous vide cooking is a brilliant way to add layer of finesse on dishes that would generally call for sashimi-style, barely cooked or canned tuna.

Serves: 4　　**Prep Time:** 10mins　　**Cook Time:** 25mins
Calories: 324　　**Protein:** 39.2g　　**Carbs:** 5.4g　　**Fat:** 15.2g

Sole Fish & Bacon

Ingredients:
-
- 10oz. sole fish fillets
- 2 tablespoons olive oil
- 2 slices bacon
- ½ tablespoon lemon juice
- Salt and pepper, to taste

Directions:
1. Preheat Sous Vide cooker to 132 degrees F.
2. Cook the bacon in a non-stick skillet and cook bacon until crispy. Remove the bacon and place aside.
3. Season fish fillets with salt, pepper, and lemon juice. Brush the fish with olive oil. Place the fish in a Sous Vide bag.
4. Top the fish with the bacon. Vacuum seal the bag. Submerge in a water bath and cook 25 minutes. Remove the fish from the bag and flash fry in a warm skillet before serving. Serve while warm.

Cook's Tip: If you are avoiding fried foods, simple serve the fish fresh out the vacuum seal bag.

Serves: 2 **Prep Time:** 10mins **Cook Time:** 25mins
Calories: 298 **Protein:** 22.4g **Carbs:** 0.4g **Fat:** 22.9g

Coriander Garlic Squids

Ingredients
-
- 4 4oz. squids, cleaned
- ¼ cup olive oil
- ¼ cup chopped coriander
- 4 cloves garlic, minced
- 2 chili peppers, chopped
- 2 teaspoons minced ginger
- ¼ cup vegetable oil
- 1 lemon, cut into wedges
- Salt and pepper, to taste

Directions
1. Set the Sous vide cooker to 136 degrees F.
2. Place the squids and 2 tablespoons olive oil in a Sous Vide bags.
3. Season to taste and vacuum seal the bag. Submerge in water and cook 2 hours.

4. Heat remaining olive oil in a skillet. Add garlic, chili pepper, and ginger and cook 1 minute. Add half the coriander and stir well.
5. Remove from the heat. Remove the squids from the bag.
6. Heat vegetable oil in a skillet, until sizzling hot. Add the squid and cook 30 seconds per side. Transfer the squids onto a plate.
7. Top with garlic-coriander mixture and sprinkle with the remaining coriander. Serve with lemon.

Cook's Tip: Squid can very easily become overcooked so keep an eye when it's close to the end of the cooking time. If you are new to Sous vide cooking, consider cooking at a lower temperature. It's always better to under cook than to overcook squid.

Serves: 4 **Prep Time:** 20min **Cook Time:** 2 hrs.
Calories: 346 **Protein:** 18.2g **Carbs:** 6.7g **Fat:** 18.56g

Swordfish Piccata

Ingredients:
-
- 2 swordfish steaks
- 1 teaspoon salt
- 1 teaspoon pepper
- 2 tablespoons olive oil
- ¼ cup butter
- 2 cloves garlic, minced
- 2 tablespoons lemon juice
- 2 tablespoons capers, with juice
- 2 tablespoons fresh basil, chopped

Directions
1. Set the sous vide machine to preheat to 140°F.
2. Season swordfish to taste, then seal into a vacuum pack bag. Place in water bath and cook 30 minutes.
3. Meanwhile, prepare the sauce. Melt butter with olive oil.

4. Add garlic and cook 30 seconds. Stir in lemon juice and capers with juice, then add basil.
5. When swordfish is cooked, transfer to plate. Serve topped with sauce.

Cook's Tip: This delicious Swordfish Piccata is best served with lemon wedges, creamy polenta and sautéed kale.

Serves: 2   **Prep Time: 20mins**   **Cook Time: 30mins**
Calories: 623   **Protein: 39.94g**   **Carbs: 3.48g**   **Fat: 49.92g**

Lazy Man's Lobster

Ingredients:
-
- Tail and claws of 1 lobster
- 2 tablespoons butter
- 1 clove garlic, minced
- ½ tablespoon fresh thyme, minced
- ¼ cup sherry
- ½ teaspoon salt
- ½ teaspoon pepper
- ¼ cup heavy cream
- Toast for serving

Directions
1. Preheat the water bath to 140°F. Seal lobster into the bag.
2. Place in water bath and cook 1 hour. Meanwhile, prepare the sauce.
3. Melt butter in a pan. Add garlic and thyme and cook 30 seconds. Add sherry and bring to a boil.

4. Remove from heat and stir in cream. Season with salt and pepper. When lobster is cooked, remove the shell and stir into sauce. Serve with toast.

Cook's Tip: Consider enhancing the lobster's flavor by testing out other ingredients in the vacuum bag. Fish stock or even brandy can be used, for example, to add an extra punch to your lobster.

Serves: 1 **Prep Time:** 20mins **Cook Time:** 1 hr.
Calories: 582 **Protein:** 26.7g **Carbs:** 5.45g **Fat:** 46.26g

Chapter 2: Sous Vide Lamb & Beef Recipes

Spiced Beef Brisket

Ingredients:
-
- 2lb. beef brisket
- Salt and pepper, to taste
- 2 tablespoons olive oil
- ½ tablespoon tomato paste
- 4 cloves garlic, minced
- 1 tablespoon smoked paprika
- ½ tablespoon beef demi-glace
- 1 teaspoon chopped thyme
- 1 cup beef stock
- ½ cup red wine
- 2 tablespoons honey
- ¾ lb. carrots, peeled, cut into matchsticks

Directions:
1. Preheat your Sous Vide cooker to 155 degrees F. Season the brisket with salt and pepper. Place the brisket into Sous Vide cooking bag.
2. Place aside. Heat ½ tablespoon olive oil in a saucepan. Add tomato paste, garlic, smoked paprika, demi-glace, thyme, stock, and wine. Simmer 5 minutes. Stir in the honey and season to taste. Simmer 1 minute. Pour the mixture into the bag with beef and vacuum seal the bag. Carefully place the bag into the cooker and cook 32 hours.
3. 25 minutes before the beef is done, toss the carrots with 1 tablespoon olive oil.
4. Roast the carrots 20-25 minutes at 450 degrees F. Remove the bag from cooker and open carefully. Strain the sauce into a small saucepot.
5. Simmer 3 minutes over medium heat. Heat the remaining olive oil in a large skillet.
6. Sear the beef 3 minutes per side. Serve the beef with roasted carrots and prepared sauce.

Cook's Tip: This fresh beef brisket is best served with creamy mashed potatoes or cauliflower mash.

Serves: 4 **Prep Time:** 20mins **Cook Time:** 32hrs.
Calories: 309 **Protein:** 18.3g **Carbs:** 20.4g **Fat:** 15.4g

Simple Spiced Ribs

Ingredients
-
- 1.5 lb. baby back ribs
- 1 tablespoon fine salt
- 1 tablespoon brown sugar
- 1 tablespoon smoked paprika
- ½ tablespoon ground cumin
- ½ tablespoon ground coriander
- ½ tablespoon black pepper
- ¼ tablespoon dried garlic
- 1 tablespoon dried parsley
- ½ cup BBQ sauce

Directions
1. Preheat Sous-vide cooker to 155 degrees F.
2. Combine all the spices and parsley in a bowl. Rub the ribs with this dry mixture.

3. Place the ribs in a Sous Vide bag and submerge in water. Cook the ribs 24 hours.
4. Remove the ribs from the bag. Preheat your grill. Cook the ribs 7-8 minutes, basting with BBQ sauce all the way.
5. Serve while hot with fresh salad.

Cook's Tip: Consider using aluminum foil to keep you produce a juicer end product and to keep the clean-up needed to a minimum.

Serves: 4 **Prep Time:** 10mins **Cook Time:** 24hrs.
Calories: 446 **Protein:** 45.3g **Carbs:** 15.6g **Fat:** 21.3g

Beef Stroganoff

Ingredients:
-
  - 1.5lb. beef loin
  - 2 sprigs thyme
  - 6 tablespoons unsalted butter
  - 2 cups sliced mushrooms
  - 6oz. wide noodles, cooked
  - 2 shallots, chopped
  - 3 teaspoons all-purpose flour
  - 1 cup beef stock
  - 2 tablespoons red wine
  - 1 cup crème Fraiche
  - Salt and pepper, to taste

Directions:
1. Preheat your Sous Vide cooker to 136 degrees F. Divide the beef among two Sous vide bags.

2. Add 2 tablespoons butter and one sprig thyme per bag. Season with salt and pepper and vacuum seal the bag.
3. Place the bags in a water bath and cook 1 hour 20 minutes.
4. Just before the meat is ready, heat 2 tablespoons butter in a skillet. Add the shallots and cook 2 minutes.
5. Toss in the mushrooms and cook 5 minutes. Stir in the flour and cook 30 seconds.
6. Add the beef stock and wine. Stir to scrape any stuck bits. Bring to a simmer.
7. Cook until slightly thickened. Stir in crème Fraiche and remove from heat.
8. Add the cooked noodles and toss to combine. Remove the beef from Sous vide bag and slice. Serve with mushrooms and noodles.

Cook's Tip: This delicious dish is best served with noodles but can also make a great addition to a side of rice.

Serves: 4 **Prep Time: 15mins** **Cook Time: 1hr. 20min**
Calories: 367 **Protein: 26.9g** **Carbs: 13.8g** **Fat: 22.1g**

Cumin-Spiced Lamb Chops

Ingredients
- 4 lamb chops
- 2 cloves garlic, mashed
- 2 teaspoons whole cumin seeds
- 2 teaspoons red pepper flakes
- 2 teaspoons coarse sea salt
- 2 teaspoons coarse pepper
- 1 tablespoon olive oil

Directions
1. Preheat the water bath to 140 degrees F.
2. Rub the lamb chops with salt, pepper, garlic, cumin, and red pepper. Seal into the bag.
3. Place in water bath and cook 2-4 hours. Remove lamb from bag and pat dry.
4. Sear on a frying pan with olive oil until brown on both sides.

Cook's Tip: This delicious dish is best served with noodles but can also make a great addition to a side of rice.

Serves: 2 **Prep Time:** 20mins **Cook Time:** 4hr. 20min
Calories: 200 **Protein:** 17.68g **Carbs:** 3.96g **Fat:** 13.12g

Sous Vide Burgers

Ingredients
- 2lb. ground beef
- 1 large egg
- 1 tablespoon dried parsley
- 1 teaspoon black pepper
- Salt, to taste

For Serving:
- Burger Buns
- Salad
- Onion rings
- Tomatoes
- Cheese Slices

Directions:
1. Heat your Sous vide cooker to 133 degrees F. In a bowl, combine beef, egg, parsley, black pepper, and desired amount of salt. Shape the mixture into patties.
2. Use a kitchen scale to portion meat into 7oz. patties.

3. Place two patties into Sous Vide Bag and vacuum seal. Cook the patties for 15 minutes up to 30 minutes.
4. Remove the patties from the cooker. Place the patties on a large plate and set aside until cooled to a room temperature.
5. Preheat your grill. Sear the patties 30 seconds per side. Serve with desired additions.

Cook's Tip: If you want your meat to be even more tender, consider wrapping in aluminum foil while resting.

Serves: 4 **Prep Time: 15mins** **Cook Time: 30mins.**
Calories: 216 **Protein: 33.2g** **Carbs: 0.5g** **Fat: 8.8g**

Sicilian Lamb Shanks

Ingredients:
-
- 1 lb. lamb shanks
- 1 teaspoon salt
- 1 teaspoon pepper
- Juice of 1 lemon
- 1 tablespoon fresh oregano, minced
- 1 clove garlic, minced
- 1 tablespoon tomato paste
- 3 roasted red peppers, mashed
- 1 bay leaf
- 1 sprig fresh rosemary
- 1 tablespoon fresh mint, chopped
- Cooked polenta, for serving

Directions
1. Preheat the water bath to 140 degrees F.

2. Make a paste of the lemon juice, oregano, garlic, tomato paste, and roasted peppers.
3. Season lamb with salt and pepper then spread paste over lamb. Seal into the bag with bay leaf and rosemary.
4. Place bag in the water bath and cook 48 hours. When the lamb is cooked, place on the bed of cooked polenta and pour sauce on top.
5. Garnish with fresh mint.

Cook's Tip: If you want your meat to be even more tender, consider wrapping in aluminum foil while resting.

Serves: 2 **Prep Time:** 20mins **Cook Time:** 48hrs.
Calories: 599 **Protein:** 101.67g **Carbs:** 13.8g **Fat:** 17.46g

Sunday Roast

Ingredients:
-
- 3lbs. chuck roast
- 2 tablespoons coarse salt
- 1 tablespoon coarse pepper
- 1 large sprig fresh rosemary
- 1 tablespoon olive oil

Directions
1. Preheat the water bath to 140 degrees F. Season the beef with salt and pepper. Seal it into a bag with the rosemary.
2. Place in water bath and cook 24 hours.
3. After 24 hours, remove beef from bag and pat dry.
4. Sear in olive oil in a hot pan until brown on all sides. Serve and enjoy!

Cook's Tip: In order to get the best eating experience, try to cook your rump to either rare or medium rare.

Serves: 6   **Prep Time: 20mins**   **Cook Time: 24hr. 20min**
Calories: 305   **Protein: 46.75g**   **Carbs: 0.74g**   **Fat: 13.01g**

Beef Wellington

Ingredients:
-
- ½ beef tenderloin, unsliced, silver skin removed
- 1 teaspoon salt
- 1 teaspoon pepper
- ¼ pound prosciutto, sliced thin
- ½ cup mushrooms, minced
- 1 shallot, minced
- ½ tablespoon tomato paste
- 2 tablespoons butter, softened
- 1 sheet refrigerated puff pastry
- 1 egg, beaten

Directions

1. Preheat the sous vide bath to 140 degrees F. Season the beef to taste then add to a vacuum seal bag.
2. Seal, and cook in bath for about an hour. Set in the refrigerator.
3. Sauté shallots in butter until translucent, then add mushrooms and sauté until cooked. Pour into a bowl and stir in tomato paste.
4. When the beef has cooled completely, preheat oven to 400 degrees F.
5. Lay puff pastry on a cutting board and spread a layer of prosciutto on top.
6. Place the chilled beef on top of the puff pastry and spread the Duxelles on all sides of the beef.
7. Wrap the prosciutto-lined pastry around the beef and seal with egg. Brush remaining egg over pastry to glaze.
8. Bake beef Wellington 15 minutes or until puff pastry is golden-brown and fully cooked. Slice across the grain to serve.

Cook's Tip: This dish is already almost complete on its own. Consider serving it with a small side salad.

Serves: 6 **Prep Time: 40mins** **Cook Time: 1hr. 15min**
Calories: 649 **Protein: 40.48g** **Carbs: 5.49g** **Fat: 13.01g**

Short Ribs Provençale

Ingredients
-
- 2 lbs. beef short ribs
- 1 teaspoon salt
- 1 teaspoon pepper
- 3 cloves garlic
- 2 sprigs fresh thyme
- 1 sprig fresh rosemary
- 2 bay leaves
- 1 tablespoon butter
- 1 tablespoon olive oil
- 1 tablespoon flour
- 2 cups red wine
- 2 cups beef stock
- 1 tablespoon tomato paste
- Crusty bread for serving

Directions
1. Preheat the water bath to 140 degrees F. Season the beef liberally with salt and pepper.
2. Place in bag with garlic, thyme, rosemary, and bay leaves. Seal and place in water bath. Cook 48 hours. 48 hours later, prepare the sauce.
3. Remove the beef from the bag and pat dry. In a Dutch oven or heavy-bottomed pan, melt butter with olive oil.
4. Add beef and sear until brown on all sides. Remove beef to a plate.
5. Stir flour into the pan and cook 30 seconds, then deglaze with wine, stirring rapidly and scraping the bottom.
6. Stir in beef stock, tomato paste, and any liquid that collected in the sous vide bag. Reduce sauce to your desired consistency. Serve over short ribs.

Cook's Tip: This dish is a perfect make ahead meal option. Simply, sous vide and braise the ribs, allow it to come to room temperature then cover and chill for up to 3 days.

Serves: 4 **Prep Time:** 30mins **Cook Time:** 48hrs. 30min
Calories: 551 **Protein:** 48.73g **Carbs:** 7.87g **Fat:** 26.82g

Rolled Beef

Ingredients:

Beef:
- 8 4oz. sliced beef
- Salt and pepper, to taste
- ¼ cup vegetable oil, to fry

Filling:
- 4oz. peas
- 1 sprig thyme
- 1 pinch sugar
- 4oz. carrots, chopped
- 8 teaspoon Dijon mustard
- 16 slices bacon

Directions:
1. Preheat Sous Vide cooker to 176 degrees F. Place the peas in a Sous Vide bag.
2. Add the carrots, a pinch of sugar and salt to taste. Vacuum seal the bag and place in a water bath. Cook the veggies 30 minutes. Remove from the bag.

3. Cover the beef slices with parchment paper. Pound with a meat tenderizer to make the beef this.
4. Spread the mustard over meat and top each slice with two pieces bacon.
5. Roll the meat into roulade, then roll the meat over veggies and secure the roulades with a kitchen twine. Season to taste.
6. Heat the oil in a skillet and sear the roulades on all sides. Cool the roulades and transfer in a Sous Vide bag.
7. Vacuum seal the beef and cook 37 hours at 153 degrees F.
8. Remove the meat from the cooker. Allow cooling completely before removing from the bag.
9. Remove the kitchen twine and slice before serving.

Cook's Tip: To enhance the flavor allow the beef to cool down to room temperature before finishing in the oven.

Serves: 8 **Prep Time: 30mins** **Cook Time: 37 hrs.**
Calories: 287 **Protein: 15.2g** **Carbs: 4.4g** **Fat: 23g**

Chapter 3: Sous Vide Summer Recipes

Crab Zucchini Roulade & Mousse

Ingredients
-
- 3lb. crab legs and claws
- 2 tablespoons olive oil
- 1 medium zucchini
- Salt and pepper, to taste

Mousse:
- 1 avocado, peeled, pitted
- 1 tablespoon Worcestershire sauce
- 2 tablespoons crème Fraiche
- 2 tablespoons fresh lime juice
- Salt, to taste

Directions:
1. Preheat Sous vide cooker to 185F. Place the claws and legs in a Sous Vide bag and vacuum seal.
2. Submerge the bag with content in a water bath. Cook the crab 10 minutes.
3. Slice the zucchini with a vegetable peeler. This way you will have some skinny strips.
4. Remove the crab from the water bath and crack the shell. Flake the meat and transfer into a bowl.
5. Add olive oil, salt, and pepper, and stir to bind gently. Make the mousse; in a food blender, blend the avocado and crème Fraiche until smooth.
6. Stir in the remaining ingredients and spoon the mixture into piping bag.
7. Arrange the zucchini slices on aluminum foil and fill with the crab meat.
8. Roll up the zucchinis and crab into a log and refrigerate 30 minutes.
9. Serve onto a plate with some avocado mousse. Enjoy.

Cook's Tip: To serve; slice the roulade into four pieces before serving and finish with a dash of salt.

Serves: 4   **Prep Time: 30mins**   **Cook Time: 10min**
Calories: 415   **Protein: 49.3g**   **Carbs: 1.6g**   **Fat: 35.5g**

Mexican Street Corn

Ingredients:
- 2 ears of corn, shucked
- 2 tbsp. cold butter
- Kosher salt
- Fresh ground pepper
- 1/4 cup mayonnaise
- 1/2 tbsp. Mexican-style chili powder
- 1/2 tsp. finely grated lime zest
- ¼ cup crumbled Cotija cheese
- ¼ cup fresh chopped cilantro
- Lime wedges, for serving

Directions:
1. Set Sous Vide Cooker to 183 degrees F.
2. Combine your butter and corn in to vacuum seal bag then set to cook in the sous vide cooker and allow it to cook for 30 minutes.
3. Combine all your remaining ingredients, except cheese, in a small bowl. Add your cheese to another plate.
4. Dip each corn ear in your mayo mixture then roll in cheese. Season to taste and enjoy!

Cook's Tip: If you find that you are having a hard time getting Cotija cheese, try substituting it for Feta as they are both Mexican and works brilliantly.

Serves: 2   **Prep Time:** 5mins   **Cook Time:** 30mins
Calories: 388   **Protein:** 10.1g   **Carbs:** 33.7g   **Fat:** 26.7g

Yukon Gold Potato Salad

Ingredients:
- 1 ½ lbs. Yukon Gold potatoes
- ½ cup chicken stock
- Salt and pepper to taste
- 4 oz. thick cut bacon, sliced
- ½ cup chopped onion
- ⅓ cup cider vinegar
- 4 scallions, thinly sliced

Directions:
1. Set Sous Vide cooker to 185F. Cut potatoes into ¾-inch thick cubes.
2. Place potatoes and chicken stock to the zip-lock bag, making sure they are in a single layer; seal using immersion water method.
3. Place potatoes in a water bath and cook for 1 hour 30 minutes.
4. Meanwhile, in last 15 minutes heat non-stick skillet over medium heat.
5. Once hot, add bacon then allow to cook until the fat renders and the bacon gets crisp; set the bacon aside and add chopped onions to the fat remaining.
6. Cook until soften for 5-7 minutes. Add vinegar and cook until reduced slightly.

7. Remove potatoes from the water bath and place them in skillet, with the cooking water.
8. Continue cooking for few minutes until liquid thickens. Remove potatoes from the heat and stir in scallions; toss to combine. Serve while still hot.

Cook's Tip: The quality of mustard really makes all the difference so try to search for a high quality whole grain mustard or even a gourmet version.

Serves: 6   **Prep Time:** 10mins   **Cook Time:** 1hrs 30mins
Calories: 108   **Protein:** 3.7g   **Carbs:** 19.9g   **Fat:** 1.6g

Radish Feta Salad

Ingredients:
- 20 small radishes, peeled, trimmed
- 1 tbsp. water
- 1 tbsp. white wine vinegar
- 1 tsp. sugar
- ¼ tsp. salt
- ½ cup feta cheese
- ¼ cup fresh spinach, chopped

Directions:
1. Preheat the water bath to 200°F. Combine the radishes, water, vinegar, sugar, and salt in a bag.
2. Seal, then place in water bath. Cook radishes 30 minutes, then place in ice water.
3. When radishes are cool, toss with cheese and basil. Serve cold.

Cook's Tip: Top this dish off with a bit of chopped mint, and lemon dressing to really enhance the flavor.

Serves: 2	**Prep Time:** 20mins	**Cook Time:** 30mins
Calories: 101	**Protein:** 5.8g	**Carbs:** 2.9g **Fat:** 7g

Aromatic Chicken

Ingredients:
- 1 cup chicken stock
- 1 tablespoon chili sauce
- 1lb. boneless chicken breasts
- 2 cloves garlic, minced
- 1 good pinch salt
- 1 lemon, thinly sliced
- 4 sprigs basil
- 1 tablespoon olive oil

Directions:
1. Combine chicken stock and chili sauce in a bowl. Add the chicken breasts and cover with a clean foil. Marinade 45 minutes.
2. In the meantime, heat the Sous Vide cooker to 146F. Pat dry the chicken with paper towels.
3. Combine the garlic and salt until you have a paste. Spread the past over chicken breasts and top the chicken with lemon.
4. Place the chicken breasts into Sous Vide bag and add-in remaining ingredients.

5. Vacuum seal the bag and submerge chicken in water. Cook the chicken 1 hour 30 minutes.
6. Heat grill pan to high. Remove the chicken from the cooker and open the bag.
7. Arrange the lemon slices on a grill pan and top with chicken. Grill the lemon and chicken for 3 minutes per side. Serve.

Cook's Tip: If you are not a huge fan of prunes consider swapping them out for apricots.

Serves: 4 **Prep Time: 20mins** **Cook Time: 1hr. 30min**
Calories: 255 **Protein: 33.3g** **Carbs: 2.2g** **Fat: 12.1g**

Mediterranean Chicken

Ingredients:
- 2 chicken breast fillets
- ½ cup sun-dried tomatoes + 2 tbsp. reserved oil
- Salt and black pepper, to taste
- 1 sprig basil
- 1 tablespoon olive oil

Directions:
1. Preheat the Sous Vide Cooker to 140 degrees F. Season the chicken with salt and pepper.
2. Heat the olive oil in a skillet. Add chicken breasts and cook for 1 minute per side.
3. Transfer immediately in Sous Vide bag and add remaining ingredients.
4. Vacuum seal the bag and submerge in water. Cook the chicken 90 minutes.
5. Remove the bag with chicken from the Cooker.
6. Open the bag and transfer the chicken to a warmed plate. Serve.

Cook's Tip: By finishing with your sun-dried tomato dressing you add a richer flavor that makes you believe that it was slow cooked with every bite.

Serves: 2 **Prep Time: 10mins** **Cook Time: 90 mins.**
Calories: 318 **Protein: 13.4g** **Carbs: 1.8g** **Fat: 29.7g**

Garlic Parmesan Broccolini

Ingredients:
- 1 bunch broccolini, washed and trimmed
- 1 tbsp. butter
- 1 clove garlic, crushed
- ¼ tsp. salt
- ¼ tsp. pepper
- 2 tbsp. grated Parmesan

Directions:
1. Preheat the water bath to 185°F. Combine broccolini, butter, garlic, salt, and pepper in a bag. Seal and place in water bath.
2. Cook 30 minutes. Remove to plate and sprinkle with Parmesan.

Cook's Tip: If you have left over Garlic Parmesan Broccolini, you can spin it into a great spaghetti dish by mixing it in with chopped eggs, pepper and spaghetti.

Serves: 4 **Prep Time:** 10mins **Cook Time:** 30mins
Calories: 62 **Protein:** 4.7g **Carbs:** 4.8g **Fat:** 3.6g

Turkey Burgers

Ingredients:
- 2lb. ground lean turkey
- 1 shallot, chopped
- ½ cup parsley, chopped
- ½ cup sun-dried tomatoes, packed in oil, chopped
- 2 cloves garlic, minced
- 1 teaspoon dry mustard powder
- 1 teaspoon paprika powder
- Salt and pepper, to taste

Directions:
1. Combine all ingredients in a bowl. Shape the mixture into 6 patties. Arrange the patties on a baking sheet lined with parchment paper.
2. Freeze 4 hours. Preheat Sous Vide cooker to 145 degrees F. Place each patty in a Sous Vide bag and vacuum seal.
3. Place in a water bath 60 minutes.
4. Remove the bag from the cooker. Open the bag and remove the patties. Heat a grill pan over medium-high heat.

5. Sear the patties for 1 minute per side. Serve with fresh salad and fresh buns.

Cook's Tip: To give your turkey burgers a nice crust, finish by coating in flour then searing on both sides.

Serves: 6 **Prep Time:** 20mins **Cook Time:** 1hr.
Calories: 212 **Protein:** 30.2g **Carbs:** 1.7g **Fat:** 9.7g

Chicken Thighs & Herbed Rice

Ingredients:
- 4 chicken thighs
- 2 tablespoons salt
- 4 cups water
- 1 tablespoon paprika powder
- 2 tablespoons vegetable oil
- 2 tablespoons butter

Herbed rice:
- ¾ cup long grain rice
- 2 cups water
- 1 teaspoon salt
- 1 bunch parsley, chopped
- 1 bunch chives, chopped

Peppers:
- 4 red bell peppers, seeded, quartered
- 3 tablespoons olive oil
- 1 sprig thyme
- Salt, to taste

Directions:
1. Make the chicken; heat Sous Vide cooker to 150 degrees F.
2. In a large bowl, combine salt and water. Add the chicken thighs to a bowl and cover with a clean foil. Refrigerate 4 hours.
3. Remove the chicken, rinse, and pat dry. Combine the butter and paprika and top the chicken.
4. Place the chicken into Sous vide bag and vacuum seal. Cook in the Sous Vide cooker 4 hours.
5. Make the peppers; combine the peppers with olive oil, thyme, and salt in a Sous Vide Bag.
6. Vacuum seal the peppers and cook in Sous Vide cooker for 30 minutes at 186 degrees F.
7. Make the rice; vacuum the rice with water, salt, and herbs. Cook in the Sous Vide cooker 60 minutes at 203 degrees F.
8. Heat vegetable oil in a skillet. Add chicken and cook until the skin is crispy.
9. Remove the peppers from the bag and cook in the same skillet with chicken, for 1 minute.
10. Spread the rice on a plate. Top with chicken and bell peppers. Serve.

Cook's Tip: To add a bit more flavor, consider swapping out salt and water in the Herbed rice with chicken broth.

Serves: 10　　**Prep Time:** 30mins　　**Cook Time:** 4hrs.
Calories: 211　　**Protein:** 9.1g　　**Carbs:** 14.8g　　**Fat:** 13.5g

Carnitas Tacos

Ingredients:
- 2 lbs. pork shoulder
- 1 teaspoon salt
- 1 teaspoon pepper
- 1 onion, chopped
- 3 cloves garlic
- ½ teaspoon ground cumin
- 2 bay leaves
- Corn tortillas for serving
- Fresh cilantro for serving
- Lime for serving

Directions:
1. Preheat the water bath to 185 degrees F. Rub pork with salt, pepper, and cumin. Seal into the bag with onion, garlic, and bay leaves.
2. Place into the water bath and cook 16 hours.

3. When pork is cooked, remove from bag and shred with two forks or your hands.
4. To serve, place a small amount of pork in a tortilla and top with cilantro and a squeeze of lime.

Cook's Tip: To enhance these tacos top with diced avocado and drizzling with a bit more lime juice.

Serves: 4 **Prep Time:** 30mins **Cook Time:** 16 hrs.
Calories: 623 **Protein:** 57.43g **Carbs:** 3.9g **Fat:** 40.24g

Chapter 4: Sous Vide Autumn/Fall Recipes

Curried Acorn Squash

Ingredients:
- 1 acorn squash, seeded and cut into wedges
- 2 tbsp. butter
- 1 tbsp. curry powder or garam masala
- ¼ tsp. salt

Directions:
1. Preheat the water bath to 185°F. Combine squash, butter, spice mix, and salt in a bag. Seal and place in water bath. Cook 1 ½ to 2 hours.

Cook's Tip: This delicious squash can be served with a variety of additions like refried beans or even a serving of stir fried vegetables.

Serves: 4 **Prep Time:** 30mins **Cook Time:** 2hrs
Calories: 99 **Protein:** 1.2g **Carbs:** 12.1g **Fat:** 6.1g

Bacon Brussels Sprouts

Ingredients:
- Brussels sprouts (1 lb., trimmed, halved)
- 2 tbsp. butter
- 2 ounces thick-cut bacon, fried and chopped
- 2 cloves garlic, minced
- ¼ tsp. salt
- ¼ tsp. pepper

Directions:
1. Preheat the water bath to 183°F. Combine all your ingredients in a large Ziploc bag.
2. Seal and place in water bath. Cook 1 hour. Meanwhile, preheat oven to 400°F. After 1 hour has passed, transfer Brussels sprouts onto a lined baking tray.
3. Set to bake until nicely roasted (about 5 minutes). Enjoy!

Cook's Tip: To enhance the flavor consider adding a bit of Apple Cider Vinegar and topping with crispy bacon bits.

Serves: 4   **Prep Time: 20mins**   **Cook Time: 1hrs 5mins**
Calories: 230   **Protein: 4g**   **Carbs: 10.8g**   **Fat: 20.2g**

Indian Style Pork

Ingredients:
- 1.5lb. pork tenderloin, sliced
- 2 cups yogurt
- 1 cup sour cream
- 2 tablespoons tandoori paste
- 1 tablespoon curry paste
- 1-inch ginger, minced
- 2 cloves garlic, minced
- Salt and pepper, to taste

Directions:
1. In a large bowl, combine yogurt, sour cream, tandoori paste, curry paste, garlic, and ginger. Add sliced pork.
2. Cover and marinate 20 minutes in a fridge. Preheat your Sous Vide cooker to 135 degrees F.
3. Remove the pork from marinade and place into Sous Vide bag. Vacuum seal the bag. Submerge pork in the water bath and cook 2 hours.

4. Remove the bag from water and open carefully. Heat 1 tablespoon olive oil in a large skillet. Sear the pork 3 minutes per side. Serve warm.

Cook's Tip: This recipe can be enhanced by adding bold ingredients such as turmeric, cumin, curry powder, garlic or even ginger.

Serves: 4   **Prep Time:** 15mins   **Cook Time:** 2 hrs.
Calories: 363   **Protein:** 12.74g   **Carbs:** 13.1g   **Fat:** 19.5g

Whiskey Infused Apples

Ingredients:
-
- 4 Gala apples
- 2 tablespoons brown sugar
- 2 tablespoons maple whiskey

Directions:
1. Preheat your Sous Vide cooker to 175F
2. Peel, core, and slice apples.
3. Place the apple slices, sugar, and whiskey into Sous Vide bag.
4. Vacuum seal and submerge in water.
5. Cook 1 hour.

Cook's Tip: These delicious apples go best with semi-sweet whipped cream.

Serves: 4 **Prep Time: 15mins** **Cook Time: 1 hr. 3 mins.**
Calories: 99 **Protein: 0.2g** **Carbs: 20.4g** **Fat: 0.5g**

Sous Vide Garlic Confit

Ingredients:

- Garlic (1 cup, cloves, peeled, minced)
- Olive oil (1/4 cup, extra virgin)
- Salt (1 tbsp.)

Directions:
1. Set your Sous Vide Cooker to preheat to 190°F.
1. Add your ingredients to a vacuum seal bag.
2. Seal and set to cook in your water bath for 4 hours.
3. To finish, transfer to an airtight container and set to refrigerate for about a month.

Cook's Tip: This garlic confit goes perfectly with pasta, toast or crackers.

Serves: 8 **Prep Time:** 10 mins **Cook Time:** 4 hrs.
Calories: 52 **Protein:** 1.1g **Carbs:** 5.6g **Fat:** 2.9g

Sweet Potato Salad

Ingredients:
- 1 ½ lbs. sweet potatoes
- ½ cup chicken stock
- Salt and pepper to taste
- 4 oz. thick cut bacon, sliced
- ½ cup chopped onion
- ⅓ cup cider vinegar
- 4 scallions, thinly sliced

Directions:
1. Set Sous Vide cooker to 185F. Cut potatoes into ¾-inch thick cubes.
2. Place potatoes and chicken stock to the zip-lock bag, making sure they are in a single layer; seal using immersion water method.
3. Place potatoes in a water bath and cook for 1 hour 30 minutes.
5. Meanwhile, in last 15 minutes heat non-stick skillet over medium heat.
6. Once hot, add bacon then allow to cook until the fat renders and the bacon gets crisp; set the bacon aside and add chopped onions to the fat remaining.
4. Cook until soften for 5-7 minutes. Add vinegar and cook until reduced slightly.
5. Remove potatoes from the water bath and place them in skillet, with the cooking water.

6. Continue cooking for few minutes until liquid thickens. Remove potatoes from the heat and stir in scallions; toss to combine.
7. Serve while still hot.

Cook's Tip: Top it off with nuts like cashews, or dried fruits like cranberries or raisins.

Serves: 4   **Prep Time: 10 mins.**   **Cook Time: 4 hrs.**
Calories: 597   **Protein: 20.1g**   **Carbs: 10.5g**   **Fat: 52.8g**

Chicken Marsala

Ingredients:
- 2 boneless, skinless chicken breasts
- 1 teaspoon salt
- 1 teaspoon pepper
- 1 lb. fresh mushrooms, sliced
- 1 shallot or ½ small onion, diced
- 2 cloves garlic, minced
- 1 cup chicken stock
- 1 cup marsala wine
- ½ tablespoon flour
- 1 tablespoon butter
- Cooked pasta for serving

Directions:
1. Preheat the water bath to 140°F.
2. Salt and pepper the chicken breasts. Place in bag and add mushrooms. Cook 2 hours.
3. When chicken is almost cooked, prepare the sauce. Melt butter in a pan and cook garlic for 30 seconds.
4. Add flour and cook until bubbling subsides, then pour in the stock wine. Cook until sauce reduces by half. Season to taste.

5. Remove the cooked chicken from the bag then slice and stir chicken and mushrooms into sauce.

Cook's Tip: Chicken Marsala goes perfectly with pasta.

Serves: 2 **Prep Time: 10 mins.** **Cook Time: 4 hrs.**
Calories: 365 **Protein: 1.3g** **Carbs: 40.1g** **Fat: 23.2g**

Warm Assorted Broccoli Salad

Ingredients:
- 3 heads broccoli, washed, chopped into florets
- 3 heads cauliflower, washed, chopped into florets
- ½ cup extra virgin olive oil, divided
- 20 cherry tomatoes, quartered
- 6 anchovy fillets, rinsed, cut into pieces
- Salt to taste
- Pepper powder to taste

Directions:
1. Fill and preheat the sous vide water bath to 183 degrees F according to the operating instructions.
2. Place the cauliflower and broccoli in a bowl. Sprinkle half the olive oil, salt, and pepper. Toss well.
3. Transfer into a Ziploc bag and vacuum-seal it.
4. Submerge the bag in the water bath and cook for 45 minutes.
5. Meanwhile place the tomatoes in a bowl. Add olives and anchovies and set aside.
6. When the vegetables are cooked, discard any liquid remaining in the pouch and transfer the vegetables into the bowl of anchovies.
7. Sprinkle the remaining olive oil. Add some salt and pepper. Toss well and serve.

Cook's Tip: Chicken Marsala goes perfectly with pasta.

Serves: 4   **Prep Time:** 10 mins.   **Cook Time:** 45 mins.
Calories: 93   **Protein:** 3.4g   **Carbs:** 9.2g   **Fat:** 5.6g

Beet Salad

Ingredients:
- Beets (2 large, sliced, peeled)
- Carrots (2 large, peeled, sliced)
- Onion (½, large, peeled, sliced)
- Potato (1 small, peeled and sliced)
- Red cabbage (¼ head, shredded)
- Stock (2 quarts)
- Dill (½ cup, chopped)
- Red wine vinegar (3 tbsp.)
- Salt and pepper to taste
- Sour cream, to serve
- Fresh dill, to serve

Directions:
1. Set your sous vide machine to 182°F. Put the beets, carrots, and onions into a vacuum-seal bag and remove all the air with a vacuum-sealer.
2. Do the same with the cabbage in a separate pouch.
3. Place the bags in the sous vide cooker for at least 1 hour. They can stay in for up to 2.
4. Remove the vegetables. Leave the cabbage to the side.

5. Bring the stock to the boil, adding the pureed vegetables, cabbage, dill, vinegar, salt and pepper. Let the soup simmer until you are ready to eat.
6. Serve the soup with a spoonful of sour cream and some fresh dill.

Cook's Tip: These delicious beets can be served with a juicy serving of steak or poultry.

Serves: 4　　**Prep Time: 10 mins.**　　**Cook Time: 15 mins.**
Calories: 77　　**Protein: 6.1g**　　**Carbs: 9.2g**　　**Fat: 2.4g**

Pumpkin Puree

Ingredients:

- 1 pumpkin, peeled and chopped
- 2 parsnips, peeled and chopped
- 1 large sweet potato, peeled and chopped
- 2 tbsp. butter
- ½ tsp. sage
- ¼ tsp. salt
- ¼ tsp. pepper

Directions:

1. Preheat oven to 185°F. Combine vegetables, butter, sage, salt, and pepper in a bag.
2. Seal and place in water bath. Cook 3 hours. Pour contents of bag into a pan. Reduce liquid to a syrup.
3. Pour the vegetables into a bowl and mash thoroughly.
4. Season to taste with additional salt, pepper, and butter if desired.

Cook's Tip: Top this off with a dash of ground cinnamon to the puree.

Serves: 3   **Prep Time: 10 mins.**   **Cook Time: 15 mins.**
Calories: 30   **Protein: 1.2g**   **Carbs: 7.5g**   **Fat: 0.12g**

Sous Vide Cauliflower Puree

Ingredients:

- 3 heads cauliflower, chopped
- 2 tbsp. butter
- ½ tsp. oregano
- ¼ tsp. salt
- ¼ tsp. pepper

Instructions:

1. Preheat sous vide oven to 185°F. Combine vegetables, butter, sage, salt, and pepper in a bag.
2. Seal and place in water bath. Cook 3 hours. Pour contents of bag into a pan. Reduce liquid to a syrup.
3. Pour the vegetables into a bowl and mash thoroughly.
4. Season to taste with additional salt, pepper, and butter if desired.

Cook's Tip: Top this off with a dash of chili pepper to the puree.

Serves: 8 **Prep Time: 10 mins.** **Cook Time: 15 mins.**
Calories: 60 **Protein: 0.9g** **Carbs: 2.4g** **Fat: 5.6g**

Chapter 5: Sous Vide Spring Recipes

Asparagus with Hollandaise

Ingredients:
- 1 bunch asparagus, trimmed
- Sous Vide Hollandaise

Directions:
1. Preheat the water bath to 145°F. Place bagged sauce in the bath.
2. Set timer for 30 minutes. When the timer has 12 minutes remaining, bag and seal asparagus.
3. Place in water bath and cook for the remaining 10-12 minutes.
4. Remove cooked asparagus from the bath. Arrange on plate. Blend sauce until smooth. Pour over asparagus.

Cook's Tip: Season Hollandaise with salt, pepper and a dash of cayenne to taste.

Serves: 4 **Prep Time:** 20 mins. **Cook Time:** 30 mins.
Calories: 347 **Protein:** 5.5g **Carbs:** 5.4g **Fat:** 34.9g

French Herb Omelet

Ingredients:
- Eggs (3 large)
- Butter (1 tbsp., unsalted, melted)
- Chives (¼ tbsp., minced)
- Parsley (¼ tbsp., minced)
- Tarragon (¼ tbsp., minced)
- Rosemary (¼ tsp., minced)
- Greek yogurt (1 tbsp., plain)
- Salt (¼ tsp.)
- Pepper (¼ tsp.)

Directions:
1. Set your sous vide machine to preheat to 165°F.
2. Add your eggs, herbs, yogurt and butter to a bowl, whisk to combine then season to taste.
3. Transfer the mixture to a vacuum seal bag and add to your water bath.
4. Allow the eggs to cook for 10 minutes. Press your eggs gently into the shape of an omelet.

5. Add the bag back into the water bath and continue to cook for another 10 minutes.
6. Transfer to a serving plate and enjoy!

Cook's Tip: This omelet can be enhanced by topping with roasted peppers and goat cheese.

Serves: 1 **Prep Time:** 10 mins. **Cook Time:** 20 mins.
Calories: 279 **Protein:** 8.9g **Carbs:** 3.4g **Fat:** 25.6g

Corn on The Cob

Ingredients:

- Corn (4 ears, shucked, washed)
- Salt, to taste
- Pepper, to taste
- Butter (4 tbsp.)
- Cilantro (1 handful, chopped)

Directions:

1. Set your sous vide machine to preheat with water to 182F.
2. Season your corn to taste then add it to your vacuum seal bag with cilantro and butter.
3. Seal, and set to cook in your sous vide bath for about 40 minutes.
4. Serve immediately.

Cook's Tip: To add even more punch to this dish throw them on the grill after removing from the sous vide bag, drizzle with lime juice and enjoy.

Serves: 4   **Prep Time: 10mins**   **Cook Time: 1 hr.**

Spicy Ginger Tofu

Ingredients:
- 1 lb. firm tofu, cut into 12 pieces
- ¼ cup soy sauce
- ¼ cup sugar
- 2 tablespoons mirin
- 2 tablespoons water
- 2 tablespoon crushed ginger
- 1 tablespoon crushed garlic
- 1 small red chili, thinly sliced

Directions:
1. Set your sous-vide machine to 180°F
2. Shallow-fry the tofu pieces until the outsides are golden brown.
3. Combine all other ingredients over a medium heat until the sugar is dissolved.
4. Place all ingredients into a Ziploc or vacuum-seal bag and seal using the water displacement method or a vacuum-sealer.

Cook's Tip: Serve this delicious dish alongside a serving of jasmine rice or mashed potatoes.

Serves: 4   **Prep Time: 10mins**   **Cook Time: 1 hr.**
Calories: 95   **Protein: 4.3g**   **Carbs: 13.5g**   **Fat: 3.6g**

Sous Vide Artichokes

Ingredients:
- Artichokes (4 whole, trimmed, halved)
- Butter (8 tbsp., unsalted)
- Garlic (8 cloves, peeled)
- Lemon zest (1 tbsp.)
- Salt
- Black pepper
- Lemon (wedges, to serve)

Directions:
1. Set your sous vide oven to preheat with water to 180°F.
2. Fill each artichoke halve with a garlic clove and a tablespoon of butter.
3. Season to taste and sprinkle with lemon zest.
4. Transfer to a vacuum sealed bag and set to cook in your sous vide machine for 2 hrs.
5. Remove from the bag, season to taste and enjoy!.

Cook's Tip: To get a more enhanced flavor for this dish consider finishing it off on the grill after brushing with olive oil.

Serves: 4 **Prep Time: 30mins** **Cook Time: 2 hrs.**
Calories: 269 **Protein: 6.7g** **Carbs: 20.1g** **Fat: 20.2g**

Cauliflower Soup

Ingredients:
- 1 large head cauliflower, break into florets
- 2 shallots, chopped
- 4 cups of vegetable stock
- ½ cup white wine
- ½ cup sour cream
- 1 ½ cups cream
- Juice of a lemon
- 1 teaspoon Ras el Hanout
- Zest of 2 lemon, grated
- A few slices roasted caraway bread
- 1 teaspoon ground cumin
- Cooking spray
- 1 cup grated cauliflower to serve
- Extra virgin olive oil to serve

Directions:
1. Place a skillet over medium heat. Spray with cooking spray. Add shallot and sauté for a couple of minutes.
2. Set your sous vide machine to 167°F. Place shallots, cauliflower, stock, wine, sour cream, cream and lemon juice into a Ziploc or a vacuum-seal bag and remove all the air with the water displacement method or a vacuum-sealer. Seal and submerge the bag in the water bath.
3. Meanwhile mix together grated cauliflower, Ras el Hanout and half of the lemon zest.
4. Remove the pouch from the cooker and transfer into blender and blend until smooth. Season with salt and pepper. Pulse a couple times to mix well.
5. Place the grated cauliflower mixture on bread slices. Drizzle some oil over it. Sprinkle salt, cumin and the remaining lemon zest.
6. Ladle into individual soup bowls.

Cook's Tip: This dish can be complemented by serving with a couple slices of toast.

Serves: 4 **Prep Time:** 15 mins. **Cook Time:** 20 mins.
Calories: 36 **Protein:** 0.2g **Carbs:** 1.1g **Fat:** 3.6g

Butter-Poached Asparagus with Fresh Mint

Ingredients:
- White asparagus (1 bunch, trimmed)
- Butter (3 tbsp., unsalted, chopped)
- Salt
- Mint (julienned)

Directions:
1. Set your sous vide oven to preheat to 185°F.
2. Add to asparagus to your vacuum seal or Ziploc bag in a flat layer then top evenly with your remaining ingredients.
3. Seal and set to cook for about 10 minutes.
4. Carefully remove from bag and serve.

Cook's Tip: When serving this delicious dish, dress it with a dash oh your melted butter from the bag and serve with your favorite potato, poultry or turkey recipe.

Serves: 2   **Prep Time:** 10 mins.   **Cook Time:** 12 mins.
Calories: 150   **Protein:** 5.7g   **Carbs:** 8.8g   **Fat:** 11.8g

Green Sesame Salad

Ingredients:
- 2 cups broccoli, snapped into small florets
- 1 cup green beans, topped and tailed
- 1 cup asparagus stems, cut in half
- 2 tablespoons soy sauce
- 1 teaspoon sesame oil
- 1 tablespoon vegetable oil
- 1 teaspoon fish sauce
- 1 handful sesame seeds
- ¼ cup scallions, finely chopped

Directions:
1. Set your sous vide machine to 180°F.
2. Place the vegetables in to a vacuum-seal bag and seal using a vacuum-sealer. Seal and submerge the bag in the water bath and cook for 10 minutes, and up to 20 if you prefer a more tender texture.
3. While vegetables are cooking, whisk together the soy sauce, sesame oil, vegetable oil and fish sauce in a small bowl
4. Put the vegetables into a large bowl and pour the dressing over, using your hands to mix everything through.

Cook's Tip: To enhance this salad consider topping with a bit of crispy bacon bits.

Serves: 4 **Prep Time:** 15 mins. **Cook Time:** 20 mins.
Calories: 115 **Protein:** 8.3g **Carbs:** 8.4g **Fat:** 5.8g

Cauliflower Alfredo

Ingredients:
- 2 cups (400g) chopped cauliflower florets
- 2 garlic cloves, crushed
- 2 tablespoons butter
- 1/2 cup double-strength chicken stock
- 2 tablespoons milk
- Salt and pepper

Directions:
1. Set your sous vide machine to 181°F.
2. Place all your ingredients into a Ziploc or vacuum-seal bag. Squeeze out some air and then fold the edge of the bag over to seal.
3. Place the bag into the prepared water bath and clip the edge to the container or pot.
4. Cook for 2 hours.
5. When ready, pour the contents of the bag into a food processor and blend until smooth and creamy.

Cook's Tip: To serve, season with more salt and pepper, and then serve over your favorite pasta.

Serves: 4 **Prep Time:** 15 mins. **Cook Time:** 20 mins.
Calories: 78 **Protein:** 1.3g **Carbs:** 5.2g **Fat:** 5.8g

Sous Vide Glazed Turnips

Ingredients:
- 1 lb. turnips, peeled and cut into chunks
- 2 tbsp. unsalted butter
- 1 tbsp. granulated sugar
- Kosher salt
- Freshly ground black pepper
- 1 tbsp. parsley, chopped

Directions:
1. Set Sous Vide machine to 183 degrees F.
2. Combine all your ingredients into a vacuum seal bad and seal.
3. Set to cook in the sous vide machine until fork tender (about 1 hr.).
4. Empty the ingredients into a skillet over medium heat and allow to reduce into a glaze. Enjoy!

Cook's Tip: To enhance the flavor top with a cube of unsalted butter while still hot.

Serves: 4 **Prep Time:** 12mins **Cook Time:** 1hr.
Calories: 100 **Protein:** 1.1g **Carbs:** 11.1g **Fat:** 6.1g

Chapter 6: Sous Vide Winter Recipes

Brussels Sprouts Sous Vide

Ingredients:
- Brussels sprouts (1 lb., trimmed, halved)
- 2 cloves garlic, minced
- ¼ tsp. salt
- ¼ tsp. pepper

Directions:
1. Preheat the water bath to 183°F. Combine all your ingredients in a large Ziploc bag.
2. Seal and place in water bath. Cook 1 hour. Meanwhile, preheat oven to 400°F. After 1 hour has passed, transfer Brussels sprouts onto a lined baking tray.
3. Set to bake until nicely roasted (about 5 minutes). Enjoy!

Cook's Tip: You can add an added layer of crunch by finishing them in a skillet with a bit of foaming butter and allowing to caramelize.

Serves: 4 **Prep Time:** 15 mins. **Cook Time:** 20 mins.
Calories: 151 **Protein:** 6.7 g **Carbs:** 9.7g **Fat:** 10.5g

Caramelized Leek & Salmon Egg Muffins

Ingredients:
- 6 eggs
- 1/2 cup unsweetened almond milk
- 2 medium leeks, thinly-sliced
- 1 tablespoon olive oil
- Pinch of salt
- 4 oz. cooked salmon
- Six 4 oz. canning jars with metal lids

Directions:
1. Set your sous vide machine to 170°F.
2. In a blender, mix the eggs and almond milk until smooth. Set aside
3. Set a skillet with oil over medium heat. Add the leeks and a pinch of salt.
4. Reduce the heat to medium and sauté until leeks soften and start to caramelize.
5. Make sure to keep stirring to prevent burning. When leeks are golden brown, remove from heat and set aside.
6. In a small bowl, combine the salmon and leeks. Stir until evenly mixed.

7. Spoon the leek mixture between the 6 jars and pour the egg mixture on top.
8. Attach the lids, keeping it loose enough to allow the air pressure to release while cooking.
9. Place in the bath and set the timer for 1 hour.
10. When ready, remove from the bath and enjoy. Leftovers can be stored in the refrigerator for up to 4 days and reheated in a toaster oven or broiler. Serve!

Cook's Tip: This dish goes perfectly with toast and avocado.

Serves: 6   **Prep Time:** 10 mins.   **Cook Time:** 1 hr. 5 mins.
Calories: 171   **Protein:** 8.3g   **Carbs:** 23.4g   **Fat:** 7.5g

Buttercup Squash Cordial

Ingredients:
- 4 small buttercup squash, peeled, seeded, chopped, juiced
- 4 cups brown sugar syrup
- 8 oz. vodka

Directions:
1. Set your sous vide machine to 148°F.
2. Place the strained buttercup squash juice and the brown sugar syrup in a Ziploc or vacuum-seal bag. Fold the top over a couple times and then clip it to your container or pot. Cook for 45 minutes.
3. Remove and place in ice water bath for 30 minutes. Remove from the ice bath and strain through a fine mesh sieve into a glass bottle.
4. In a shaker, add the butternut squash syrup and then the vodka. Shake well to mix and serve over ice. Syrup can be refrigerated for up to 2 weeks.

Cook's Tip: To enhance the flavor add a splash of cider vinegar and lemon juice.

Serves: 4 **Prep Time:** 20 mins. **Cook Time:** 5 hrs.
Calories: 116 **Protein:** 9.3g **Carbs:** 19.2g **Fat:** 2g

Delicata Squash Puree

Ingredients:

- 1 Delicata Squash, peeled and chopped
- 2 tbsp. butter
- ½ tsp. sage
- ¼ tsp. salt
- ¼ tsp. pepper

Directions:

1. Preheat oven to 185°F. Combine squash, butter, sage, salt, and pepper in a bag.
2. Seal and place in water bath. Cook 3 hours. Pour contents of bag into a pan. Reduce liquid to a syrup.
3. Pour the vegetables into a bowl and mash thoroughly.
4. Season to taste with additional salt, pepper, and butter if desired.

Cook's Tip: Top this off with a dash of ground cinnamon to the puree.

Serves: 3　　**Prep Time:** 10 mins.　　**Cook Time:** 15 mins.
Calories: 30　　**Protein:** 1.2g　　**Carbs:** 7.5g　　**Fat:** 0.12g

Leek Salad

Ingredients:
- 2 large leeks, peeled and sliced
- ½ large onion, peeled and sliced
- 2 quarts stock of your choice
- ½ cup chopped fresh dill
- 3 tablespoons red wine vinegar
- Salt and pepper to taste
- Sour cream, to serve
- Fresh dill, to serve

Directions:
1. Allow your sous vide machine to preheat to 182°F.
2. Put the leeks, and onions into a vacuum-seal bag and seal with a vacuum-sealer. Do the same with the cabbage in a separate pouch.
3. Place the bags in the sous vide cooker for at least 1 hour. They can stay in for up to 2.
4. Remove the vegetables. Leave the cabbage to the side.
5. Bring the stock to the boil, adding the pureed vegetables, cabbage, dill, vinegar, salt and pepper. Let the soup simmer until you are ready to eat.
6. Serve the soup with a spoonful of sour cream and some fresh dill.

Cook's Tip: This delicious salad can be served with a juicy serving of steak or poultry.

Serves: 4   **Prep Time:** 10 mins.   **Cook Time:** 15 mins.
Calories: 77   **Protein:** 6.1g   **Carbs:** 9.2g   **Fat:** 2.4g

Sweet Potato Soup

Ingredients:
- 1 lb. sweet potato, peeled, cubed
- 2 shallots, chopped
- 4 cups of vegetable stock
- ½ cup white wine
- ½ cup sour cream
- 1 ½ cups cream
- Juice of a lemon
- Zest of 2 lemon, grated
- 1 teaspoon ground cumin
- Cooking spray
- Extra virgin olive oil to serve

Directions:
1. Place a skillet over medium heat. Spray with cooking spray. Add shallot and sauté for a couple of minutes.
2. Set your sous vide machine to 167°F. Place shallots, sweet potato, stock, wine, sour cream, cream and lemon juice into a vacuum-seal bag and seal with a vacuum-sealer. Submerge the bag in the water bath.
3. Meanwhile mix together sweet potato puree and half of the lemon zest.
4. Remove the pouch from the cooker and transfer into blender and blend until smooth. Season with salt and pepper. Pulse a couple times to mix well.

5. Drizzle some oil over it. Sprinkle salt, cumin and the remaining lemon zest.
6. Ladle into individual soup bowls.

Cook's Tip: This sweet potato soup can be enhanced by adding a dash of heavy cream before drizzling with oil. Then serve by topping with crumbled bacon.

Serves: 4 **Prep Time:** 25 mins. **Cook Time:** 45 mins.
Calories: 108 **Protein:** 1.8g **Carbs:** 25.6g **Fat:** 0.14g

Miso-Butter Japanese Turnips

Ingredients:
- Water (2 tbsp.)
- Butter (2 tbsp., unsalted, cubed)
- Miso (2 tbsp., white, dissolved in warm water)
- Sugar (1/2 tsp., granulated)
- Japanese turnips (1 lb., trimmed, washed)

Directions:
1. Set Sous Vide machine to 183 degrees F.
2. Combine all your ingredients into a vacuum seal bad and seal.
3. Set to cook in the sous vide machine until fork tender (about 1 hr.).
4. Empty the ingredients into a skillet over medium heat and allow to reduce into a glaze. Enjoy!

Cook's Tip: Top this dish off with some green onion slices and enjoy on it's own or with a few slices of bread.

Serves: 4   **Prep Time: 30 mins.**   **Cook Time: 1 hr.**
Calories: 85   **Protein: 2.3g**   **Carbs: 9.9g**   **Fat: 0.14g**

Pickled Fennel Salad

Ingredients:
- 1 bulb of fennel, thinly sliced
- ½ tsp yellow mustard seeds
- ½ cup white wine vinegar
- 1 tablespoon fine sugar
- 2 sweet oranges, sliced into thin wedges
- Fennel fronds (if on hand)
- Fresh parsley, roughly chopped
- Sea salt flakes
- Olive oil, to serve

Directions:
1. Set your sous vide machine to 180°F.
2. Dissolve the sugar in the vinegar by heating it gently in a saucepan. Allow to cool.
3. Place the fennel, mustard seeds, and vinegar mixture into a Ziploc or vacuum-seal bag. Remove all the air with the water displacement method or a vacuum-sealer.
4. Place into your water bath for 30 minutes.

5. Remove the fennel from the pickling liquid and toss with orange, fennel fronds, and parsley. Drizzle with olive oil, add salt to taste, and serve.

Cook's Tip: To a bit more texture consider topping with crispy bacon.

Serves: 4 **Prep Time:** 15 mins. **Cook Time:** 1 hr.
Calories: 349 **Protein:** 6.6g **Carbs:** 13.3g **Fat:** 31.3g

Rosemary & Lemon-Infused Salmon

Ingredients:
- 4 lbs. wild salmon
- 2 Tablespoons olive oil
- 1 Tablespoon rosemary, chopped
- Zest of one lemon
- Juice of one lemon
- ¼ teaspoon garlic powder
- ¼ teaspoon black pepper
- ⅛ teaspoon sea salt
- 2 cloves garlic, thinly sliced
- 2 tablespoons capers

Directions:
1. Set your sous vide machine to 115°F.
2. In a small bowl, whisk together the olive oil, rosemary, lemon juice, zest, salt, pepper, and garlic powder.
3. Place the salmon into a vacuum-seal bag and seal with a vacuum-sealer.
4. Set to cook in your water bath for about 30 minutes
5. When ready, remove from the bath and pour the contents onto a shallow soup bowl or a plate with a lip to keep the juices.

6. Set a skillet with oil over medium heat. Once hot, sauté the garlic until fragrant and crisp. Remove the garlic with the slotted spoon.
7. In the pan, sear the salmon pieces, skin side down, for 3 minutes or until skin is crispy.
8. Remove the salmon from the pan and garnish with the crispy garlic slices and capers.

Cook's Tip: This delicious salmon is best served with mashed potatoes and green beans.

Serves: 4 **Prep Time: 15 mins.** **Cook Time: 33 mins.**
Calories: 517 **Protein: 26.9g** **Carbs: 58.7 g** **Fat: 25.6g**

Chapter 7: Sous Vide Poultry Recipes

Chicken Wings

Ingredients:
- 12 chicken wings
- ¼ cup vegetable oil
- 4 sprigs thyme
- 2 teaspoons crushed red pepper flakes
- Salt, to taste

Directions:
1. Preheat Sous Vide cooker to 167F.
2. In a Sous Vide bag, combine the chicken wing with remaining ingredients.
3. Shake gently to coat the chicken and vacuum seal the bag.
4. Submerge in water and cook 7 hours.
5. Remove the bag with chicken from cooker. Heat some oil in a large skillet.
6. Place the wings into a skillet and cook until the skin is crispy. Serve.

Cook's Tip: Top these wings with delicious blue cheese dressing to get an extra level of flavor.

Serves: 4   **Prep Time: 20mins**   **Cook Time: 7 hrs.**
Calories: 361   **Protein: 14.7g**   **Carbs: 8.6g**   **Fat: 29.8g**

Fried Chicken

Ingredients:
Chicken:
- 3 lb. chicken drums
- 1 tbsp. fine salt

Coating:
- 3 cups all-purpose flour
- 1 tbsp. onion powder
- 1 tsp. garlic powder
- ½ tbsp. dried basil
- 1 tbsp. salt
- 2 cup buttermilk

Directions:
1. Preheat Sous Vide cooker to 155F. Season chicken with salt. Place the chicken drums in Sous Vide bags.
2. Vacuum seal. Submerge in water and cook 2 hours. Heat 3-inches oil in a pot.
3. Remove the chicken from bags and pat dry. Combine all dry breading ingredients in a large bowl. Place buttermilk in a separate bowl.
4. Dredge chicken drums in flour, buttermilk, and flour again. Fry chicken in batches, until golden and crispy.

5. Serve warm with fresh salad and favorite sauce.

Cook's Tip: Crispy bacon, sautéed onion, ham, and garlic perfect these collard greens, making them an essential part.

Serves: 8   **Prep Time: 15mins**   **Cook Time: 2hrs**
Calories: 357   **Protein: 28.4g**   **Carbs: 39.6g**   **Fat: 10g**

Sticky Duck Wings

Ingredients:
- 3lb. duck wings
- 1 tbsp. mustard
- ½ cup honey
- 1 tbsp. soy sauce
- ¼ cup ketchup
- 1 tbsp. hot sauce
- 2 tbsp. Cajun spice blend
- ¼ cup butter
- Salt and pepper, to taste

Directions:
1. Preheat Sous Vide cooker to 150F. Cut the wings into portions and rub with Cajun blend.
2. Season with some salt and pepper. Transfer the wings into cooking bags and add butter.
3. Vacuum seal the wings and submerge in water. Cook the wings 2 hours. Preheat your broiler.
4. Combine remaining ingredients in a bowl. Remove the wings from the cooker and toss with prepared sauce.

5. Arrange the wings on baking sheet and broil 10 minutes, basting with any remaining sauce during that time. Serve warm.

Cook's Tip: You can add a fuller flavor by cooking in duck fat instead of olive oil.

Serves: 6   **Prep Time: 20mins**   **Cook Time: 2hrs**
Calories: 305   **Protein: 15.8g**   **Carbs: 27g**   **Fat: 16.1g**

Sage Infused Turkey

Ingredients:
- 2 turkey legs and thighs, with bone and skin
- 1 lemon, sliced
- 10 sage leaves
- 4 cloves garlic, halved
- Salt, to taste
- 1 teaspoon black peppercorns

Directions:
1. Preheat Sous Vide bath to 148 degrees F. Season the turkey to taste, then add to a vacuum seal bag with all your remaining ingredients.
2. Seal, and set to cook in the sous vide machine for 12 hours on the turkey related settings.
3. Dry Turkey, and pan sear on medium until lightly browned on all sides then serve.

Cook's Tip: To achieve a moister turkey, consider basting it with mayonnaise.

Serves: 6 **Prep Time: 10mins** **Cook Time: 12 hrs.**
Calories: 310 **Protein: 57.9g** **Carbs: 2.6g** **Fat: 6.4g**

Chicken Cordon Bleu

Ingredients:
- 2 boneless, skinless chicken breasts, butterflied
- 4 deli slices ham
- 4 deli slices Swiss cheese
- ½ cup flour
- 1 egg
- 1 cup bread crumbs
- 1 cup vegetable oil

Directions:
1. Preheat the water bath to 140°F. Lay slices of ham on top of butterflied chicken breasts, then lay cheese on top of ham.
2. Trim excess. Roll up chicken breasts with the ham and cheese on the inside.
3. Place prepared chicken breasts inside the bag. Seal tightly and place in water bath. Cook 1 ½ hours.
4. When chicken is done, remove carefully from wrapper and pat dry. Dredge each piece in flour, then dip in egg, followed by the breadcrumbs. Heat oil to 350°F.
5. Fry chicken until golden brown on all sides.
6. Remove to paper towel to drain. Cut breasts in halves, then serve.

Cook's Tip: Enhance the flavor by adding a bit of parsley, thyme, and dried mustard.

Serves: 4 **Prep Time:** 30mins **Cook Time:** 1hr 30mins
Calories: 567 **Protein:** 46.2g **Carbs:** 34.2g **Fat:** 26g

Duck a la Orange

Ingredients:
- 2 5oz. duck breast fillets, skin on
- 1 orange, sliced
- 4 cloves garlic
- 1 shallot, chopped
- 4 sprigs thyme
- 1 teaspoon black peppercorns
- 1 tablespoon sherry vinegar
- ¼ cup red wine
- 2 tablespoons butter
- Salt, to taste

Directions:
1. Preheat Sous Vide cooker to 135 degrees F. Place the duck breast fillets into a Sous Vide bag.
2. Top the breasts with orange slices, garlic, shallot, thyme, and peppercorns. Vacuum seal the bag and submerge in water. Cook the breasts 2 ½ hours.
3. Remove the bag from a water bath.
4. Open the bag and remove the breasts. Heat a large skillet over medium-high heat. Sear the duck, skin side down, for 30 seconds.

5. Place the breasts aside and keep warm. In the same skillet, add sherry vinegar and wine.
6. Add the bag content and bring to simmer. Simmer 5 minutes.
7. Stir in the butter and simmer 1 minute. Serve the duck with prepared sauce.

Cook's Tip: Feel free to substitute for blood oranges and cranberry juice to enhance the flavor of this recipe.

Serves: 2   **Prep Time: 20mins**   **Cook Time: 2hrs 30 mins.**
Calories: 466   **Protein: 34.5g**   **Carbs: 15.1g**   **Fat: 27.4g**

Sweet Chicken Teriyaki

Ingredients:
- 2 chicken breasts, skinless, boneless, cleaned, pat dried
- 2 teaspoons sugar
- 1 teaspoon salt
- 4 tablespoons soy sauce
- 4 tablespoons sake
- 1 tablespoon ginger juice

Directions:
1. Brush the chicken pieces with ginger juice. Mix together salt and half the sugar in a small bowl. Sprinkle this mixture on both sides of the chicken.
2. Place the chicken pieces into a vacuum-seal bag and seal. Set aside to marinate for at least 3 – 5 hours.
3. Set your sous vide machine to 140°F.
4. Submerge the bag of chicken in to the water bath and cook for 1 ½ hours or until the chicken is done.
5. Carefully open the bag and remove the chicken.
6. Pat dry with paper towels.

7. Pour the cooking liquid into a small saucepan. Add sake, soy sauce and remaining sugar. Place the saucepan over medium heat and simmer until the sauce has reduced to a syrup.
8. Spread half the sauce over the chicken and place the chicken under the broiler until caramelized.
9. Remove from the broiler and drizzle the remaining sauce and serve.

Cook's Tip: This dish is best served with Jasmine rice.

Serves: 2   **Prep Time:** 20mins   **Cook Time:** 2hrs.
Calories: 259   **Protein:** 42.5g   **Carbs:** 12.6g   **Fat:** 4.9g

Fresh Chicken Salad

Ingredients:
- 1-pound bone–in, skinned chicken breast halves
- 1 lemon, sliced
- Zest of half a lemon, grated
- 1 tablespoon lemon juice
- 1 small red onion, finely chopped
- 1 stalk celery, finely chopped
- 2 cloves garlic, minced
- 2 whole sprigs tarragon
- 1 tablespoon fresh tarragon leaves, minced
- 2–3 tablespoons mayonnaise or to taste
- ½ tablespoon Dijon mustard or to taste
- Kosher salt to taste
- Pepper powder to taste
- 2 teaspoons fresh parsley leaves, minced
- 2 teaspoons fresh chives, minced
- Lettuce leaves to serve

Directions:
1. Allow your sous vide machine to preheat to 150°F.
2. Sprinkle salt and pepper over the chicken breasts. Place the chicken pieces into a bag and seal. Submerge the bag in the water bath and allow to cook for about 4 hours or until done.
3. When done, remove the bag from the water bath and place on an ice bath to chill.
4. When cool enough to handle, remove the skin and bones from the chicken and discard it. Chop the chicken into bite sized pieces
5. Add zest, lemon juice, mustard, mayonnaise, minced tarragon, parsley, chives, onions, celery and garlic to a large bowl. Whisk well.
6. Add chicken pieces, salt and pepper. Fold until well combined.
7. Serve over a bed of lettuce leaves. Enjoy!

Cook's Tip: This salad is delicious on its own but you can enhance the flavors a tad by topping with grated parmesan cheese.

Serves: 4   **Prep Time: 10mins**   **Cook Time: 4hrs**
Calories: 212   **Protein: 25.8g**   **Carbs: 12.6g**   **Fat: 6.7g**

Viet-Style Chicken Skewers

Ingredients
- 1 lb. chicken breast or thighs, chopped into 1-inch pieces
- 1 stalk fresh lemongrass, chopped and smashed
- 2 Tablespoons fish sauce
- 2 Tablespoons coconut sugar
- 1/2 teaspoon salt
- 1 tablespoon chili-garlic sauce

Directions
1. Set your sous vide machine to 150°F.
2. In a blender, combine the lemongrass, sugar, fish sauce, and salt. Process until ingredients are mixed and lemongrass finely chopped.
3. In a medium sized bowl, add your chicken pieces and pour the marinade over the chicken. Set aside to marinate in the refrigerator for at least 20 min.
4. When ready, skewer 3 - 4 pieces of chicken on each skewer, making sure to cushion the pointy end of the skewer with a piece of chicken.
5. Place the skewers into a bag. Pour in the remaining marinade.
6. Seal and set to cook for about 45 minutes.
7. When the chicken is ready, remove from the bath and brush with chili garlic sauce. Place the skewers onto a baking sheet and broil for a few minutes.

Cook's Tip: If you do not have access to a broiler, a grill or backyard barbecue will also achieve the same delicious outcome.

Serves: 4 **Prep Time:** 10mins **Cook Time:** 1 hr.
Calories: 244 **Protein:** 25.8g **Carbs:** 13.2g **Fat:** 10.4g

Curry Chicken Soup

Ingredients:
2 cups diced celery
(4-pound) whole chicken, trussed
6 cups water
2 cups diced white onion
Salt and Black pepper
1 tablespoon coconut oil
1 cup thinly sliced shallots
2 tablespoons red curry paste
1 tablespoon curry powder
2 garlic cloves, minced
1 teaspoon ground turmeric
2 cups diced carrots
1 teaspoon ground coriander
1 teaspoon sugar
1/2 teaspoon crushed red pepper
4 cups fresh spinach leaves
1/4 cup thinly sliced scallions
1 tablespoon fish sauce
Cilantro and lime wedges, for serving

Directions:

1. Set your sous vide machine to 150°F.
2. In a large zip lock or vacuum-seal bag, combine the onion, celery, carrots, water and chicken. Season to taste.
Seal and set to cook for about 6 hours. Use plastic wrap to cover the sous vide water bath to help prevent evaporation. Continuously top up the pot of water to keep the chicken fully submerged.
3. Strain the soup through a fine mesh strainer then discard the rest of the vegetables.
4. Let the chicken rest until cool to the touch, then remove and shred the meat.
5. Set a stockpot with oil over medium heat. Add shallots then cook, while stirring, until soft.
6. Add red pepper, sugar, coriander, turmeric, garlic, curry powder and curry paste. Continue to cook for 5 minutes, and then add reserved cooking liquid and bring to a simmer. Continue to simmer for 30 minutes to allow the flavors to meld.
7. Near the end of the cooking process, add the chicken, fish sauce, spinach, and scallions.
Simmer until heated through and the spinach has wilted, about 2 minutes. Season to taste. Serve. topped with cilantro and lime wedges.

Cook's Tip: Best served with a serving of crackers.

Serves: 4   **Prep Time:** 10mins   **Cook Time:** 4hrs
Calories: 147.2   **Protein:** 16g   **Carbs:** 7.6g   **Fat:** 5.1g

Chapter 8: Sous Vide Pork Recipes

Pulled Pork

Ingredients:
- 2lb. pork shoulder, trimmed
- 1 tablespoon ketchup
- 4 tablespoons Dijon mustard
- 2 tablespoons maple syrup
- 2 tablespoons soy sauce

Directions:
1. Preheat your Sous Vide cooker to 158 degrees F.
2. In a bowl, combine ketchup, mustard, maple syrup, and soy sauce. Place the pork with prepared sauce into Sous Vide bag.
3. Vacuum seal the bag and submerge in water. Cook the pork 24 hours.
4. Open the bag and remove pork. Strain cooking juices into a saucepan. Torch the pork to create a crust.
5. Simmer the cooking juices in a saucepan until thickened.
6. Pull pork before serving. Serve with thickened sauce.

Cook's Tip: This pulled pork makes killer lunch sandwiches!

Serves: 6   **Prep Time: 10mins**   **Cook Time: 24 hrs.**
Calories: 471   **Protein: 36g**   **Carbs: 6.1g**   **Fat: 32.8g**

Breakfast Sausage Patties

Ingredients:

- 1 lb. ground pork
- 1 teaspoon salt
- ½ teaspoon pepper
- 1 clove garlic, minced
- ½ onion, minced
- ½ teaspoon dried thyme
- ½ teaspoon dried rosemary
- ½ teaspoon dried sage
- ½ teaspoon dried parsley
- 1 egg
- 1 tablespoon olive oil

Directions:
1. Preheat the water bath to 140 degrees F. Mash together all ingredients in a bowl.
2. Place in bag and press to fill all corners in a flat patty. Seal bag, place in the water bath and cook 2 hours.
3. When pork is cooked, cut off the bag.
4. Cut patty into squares. Immediately before serving, heat oil in a pan. Sear patties in oil until brown on both sides. Serve.

Cook's Tip: Consider using these succulent patties in breakfast sandwiches.

Serves: 4   **Prep Time:** 20mins   **Cook Time:** 20 hrs. 20 min
Calories: 407   **Protein:** 34.64g   **Carbs:** 2.14g   **Fat:** 29.39g

Tokyo-Style Pork Ramen

Ingredients:
- ½ pound pork belly
- ¼ cup brown sugar
- ¼ cup soy sauce
- ¼ cup dry sherry
- For soup:
- 3 cups chicken broth
- 1 teaspoon sugar
- 1 tablespoon dry sherry
- 3 tablespoons soy sauce
- 2 packages fresh ramen noodles
- 2 scallions, sliced

Directions:
1. Preheat the water bath to 170°F.
2. Combine sugar, soy sauce, and sherry.
3. Spread over pork. Seal into bag, place in the water bath, and cook 10 hours. ½ hour before pork is cooked, prepare the soup.
4. In a pot, combine chicken broth, sugar, sherry, and soy sauce. Season to taste.

5. Cook ramen noodles according to package instructions. Divide noodles and broth between two bowls.
6. When pork is cooked, slice into ½-inch thick pieces. Divide between bowls of ramen and top with scallion.

Cook's Tip: Spice this dish up a bit by adding a dash of smoked paprika into the mix.

Serves: 2 **Prep Time:** 30mins **Cook Time:** 10 hrs.
Calories: 1140 **Protein:** 26.1g **Carbs:** 83.19g **Fat:** 75.48g

Pork Knuckles

Ingredients:
- 2 10oz. pork knuckles
- Salt and pepper, to taste
- 4 cloves garlic, chopped
- ½ cup mustard
- ½ cup raw apple cider vinegar
- 2 ¾ cups apple juice
- ½ cup brown sugar
- 4 sprigs thyme
- 1 bay leaf

Directions:
1. Preheat Sous Vide cooker to 158 degrees F. Generously season pork knuckles with salt and pepper. Heat some oil in a large skillet. Sear pork 2 minutes per side.
2. Remove from the skillet. Toss the remaining ingredients into a skillet, and cook until reduced by half. Place aside to cool.
3. Place the pork knuckles in Sous Vide bag along with the prepared sauce. Vacuum seal the bag. Submerge bag in a water bath. Cook 24 hours.
4. Remove shanks from the bag and place aside. Strain cooking juices into a saucepan.

5. Simmer over medium heat until thickened. Pour the sauce over shanks and serve.

Cook's Tip: To add another level of texture, consider searing slightly.

Serves: 4 **Prep Time:** 20mins **Cook Time:** 24 hrs.
Calories: 358 **Protein:** 24.9g **Carbs:** 45.2g **Fat:** 8.6g

Pork Medallions

Ingredients:
- 1 tablespoon olive oil
- 1 pinch salt
- 1 pinch black pepper
- 1 teaspoon ground cumin
- ¼ cup chopped fresh parsley
- 1 ¾ lb. pork tenderloin

Directions:
1. Preheat the Sous Vide cooker to 145 degrees F. Cut the pork tenderloin in medallions.
2. Season with salt, pepper, and cumin. Place the seasoned pork into Sous Vide bag and add parsley. Vacuum seals the bag and submerge in water.
3. Cook the medallions 1 hour.
4. Heat olive oil in a large skillet. Remove the medallions from the cooker.
5. Sear on both sides. Serve warm.

Cook's Tip: Drizzling the finished product with a bit of unsalted butter to add a whole new layer of flavor.

Serves: 4 **Prep Time:** 10mins **Cook Time:** 1 hr.
Calories: 317 **Protein:** 52.1g **Carbs:** 0.5g **Fat:** 10.6g

Barbecue Ribs

Ingredients:
- 1 rack pork ribs
- 1 tablespoon salt
- 1 teaspoon pepper
- 2 tablespoons brown sugar
- 1 tablespoon garlic powder
- 1 tablespoon onion powder
- 2 tablespoons paprika
- ½ cup barbecue sauce, plus extra for serving

Directions:
1. Preheat the water bath to 165 degrees F.
2. Combine salt, pepper, sugar, garlic powder, onion powder, and paprika.
3. Rub all over ribs. Seal ribs into bag and place in water bath. Cook 12 hours.
4. When ribs are cooked, place on a baking sheet lined with aluminum foil.
5. Spread barbecue sauce over ribs. Place under broiler until sauce bubbles.
6. Serve with additional sauce.

Cook's Tip: These ribs go best with a fresh garden salad.

Serves: 4 **Prep Time:** 20mins **Cook Time:** 12 hrs.
Calories: 579 **Protein:** 72.06g **Carbs:** 23.99g **Fat:** 19.91g

BLT

Ingredients:
- 1 package thick-cut bacon in original vacuum-sealed packaging
- 6 slices bread, toasted
- 6 slices tomato
- 3 leaves lettuce
- 3 tablespoons mayonnaise

Directions:
1. Preheat the water bath to 140 degrees F. Place sealed bacon in the water bath.
2. Cook at least 4 hours or overnight. After at least 4 hours, remove bacon from pan.
3. Brown in the hot pan on both sides. Drain on paper towel.
4. Spread mayonnaise on bread. Assemble sandwiches with tomato and lettuce. Serve.

Cook's Tip: Adding a splash of liquid spoke into the bag before sealing will add a more of a BBQ feel to your BLT.

Serves: 3 **Prep Time: 20mins** **Cook Time: 4 hrs. 20 min**
Calories: 812 **Protein: 22.74g** **Carbs: 22.56g   Fat: 70.07g**

Pork Osso Bucco

Ingredients:
- 2 pork shanks
- 1 tablespoon olive oil
- ½ sweet onion, finely chopped
- 1 carrot, finely chopped
- 1 stalk celery, finely chopped
- 4 cloves garlic, minced
- 1 teaspoon salt
- 1 teaspoon pepper
- ½ cup white wine
- 7 oz. whole tomatoes, crushed
- 2 bay leaves
- 2 sprigs rosemary
- 2 sprigs thyme
- Crusty bread for serving

Directions:
1. Preheat the water bath to 175 degrees F. Meanwhile, prepare the sauce.
2. Heat 1 tablespoon olive oil in a saucepan. Add onions, carrots, and celery and cook until onion is translucent.
3. Add garlic and stir. Pour in wine and tomatoes and cook until sauce is reduced and alcohol smell has evaporated.
4. Remove from heat.
5. Season the shanks with salt and pepper. Place each shank into a separate bag and add half the sauce to each bag. Divide the herbs between the bags.
6. Seal and place into the water bath. Cook for 24 hours.

Cook's Tip: This pork recipe goes perfectly with a bit of crusty bread.

Serves: 2 **Prep Time: 30mins** **Cook Time: 24 hrs.**
Calories: 683 **Protein: 102.2g** **Carbs: 18.25g** **Fat: 20.71g**

Spiced Pork Loin Steaks

Ingredients:

- 1 - 1.5 lbs. pork loin, cut into 4 steaks
- 1 Tablespoon cocoa powder
- 1 teaspoon chipotle chili powder
- 1 teaspoon garlic powder
- 1 teaspoon ground cumin
- ½ teaspoon cinnamon
- ½ teaspoon salt
- 8 oz. onion, chopped
- ¾ oz. poblano pepper, chopped finely
- 2 tablespoons olive oil
- 1 can pineapple

Directions:

1. Set your sous vide machine to 145°F.
2. Lay the pork steaks onto a clean chopping board to dry. Meanwhile, combine all the dry spices to make a spice mix.
3. Rub the steak with the spice mix until completely coated. Coat each steak or chop completely with the rub

4. Place the steaks or chops in a Ziploc bag or vacuum-seal bag and remove the air via the water displacement method or vacuum-sealer.
5. Submerge in the heated water bath and set the timer for 1 hour.
6. When steaks are ready, remove the steaks and pat dry with clean paper towels.
7. Heat a skillet and sear each side of the steaks until crispy. Let the steaks rest for a minute before serving with the sauce.

Sauce:

1. Set a skillet with oil over medium heat. When hot, add the pepper and onion, season to taste and sauté until caramelized.
2. Add pineapple and continue to cook until liquid has evaporated.
3. Transfer the mixture to a blender and puree until smooth.

Cook's Tip: This goes best with rice, asparagus or potatoes.

Serves: 4 **Prep Time: 30mins** **Cook Time: 2 hrs.**
Calories: 154 **Protein: 23.29g** **Carbs: 1.5g** **Fat: 6.13g**

Honey Mustard Pork Shoulder

Ingredients:
- 2lb. pork shoulder, trimmed
- 1 tablespoon ketchup
- 4 tablespoons Dijon mustard
- 4 tablespoons honey
- 2 tablespoons soy sauce

Directions:
1. Preheat your Sous Vide cooker to 158 degrees F.
2. In a bowl, combine ketchup, mustard, maple syrup, and soy sauce. Place the pork with prepared sauce into Sous Vide bag.
3. Vacuum seal the bag and submerge in water. Cook the pork 24 hours.
4. Open the bag and remove pork. Strain cooking juices into a saucepan. Torch the pork to create a crust.
5. Simmer the cooking juices in a saucepan until thickened.
6. Serve with thickened sauce.

Cook's Tip: This recipe is best served with a fluffy plate of Basmati rice.

Serves: 6 **Prep Time: 10mins** **Cook Time: 24 hrs.**
Calories: 471 **Protein: 36g** **Carbs: 6.1g** **Fat: 32.8g**

Chapter 9: Sous Vide Marinades & Sauces Recipes

Béarnaise Sauce

Ingredients:
- ¼ cup white wine
- 2 sprigs fresh tarragon
- 1 shallot, minced
- 2 egg yolks
- ¼ cup butter
- ½ teaspoon salt
- ½ teaspoon pepper

Directions:
1. Preheat the water bath to 170°F.
2. Combine all ingredients in a bag and seal.
3. Place in water bath and cook 1 hour.
4. Remove tarragon sprigs. Blend until smooth.

Cook's Tip: This delicious sauce goes well with fish or plain meat.

Serves: 2   **Prep Time:** 20mins   **Cook Time:** 1 hr.
Calories: 288   **Protein:** 3.16g   **Carbs:** 3.9g   **Fat:** 27.58g

Hollandaise Sauce

Ingredients:
- 1 ½ cups butter
- 4 egg yolks
- ½ cup water
- 2 ½ tablespoons white wine vinegar
- 1 teaspoon salt

Directions:
1. Preheat Sous Vide cooker to 167F. Whisk all ingredients in a bowl.
2. Pour the sauce into Sous Vide bag and seal the bag using water immersion technique.
3. Submerge sauce in water and cook 30 minutes.
4. Remove the bag from the cooker. Open the bag and transfer the bag content into a bowl. Whisk 30 seconds using an electric whisk. Serve.

Cook's Tip: This sauce is delicious over poached eggs as you would in an Eggs Benedict.

Serves: 8   **Prep Time: 5mins**   **Cook Time: 30mins**
Calories: 332   **Protein: 1.7g**   **Carbs: 0.3g**   **Fat: 36.8g**

Tomato Sauce

Ingredients:
- 2 tablespoons olive oil
- 2 onions, chopped
- 2 cloves garlic, minced
- 2lb. cherry tomatoes
- 2 sprigs fresh basil
- 3 sprigs fresh oregano
- 1/3 cup fresh chopped parsley
- Salt, to taste

Directions:
1. Preheat Sous vide cooker to 180F. Heat olive oil in a skillet. Add onions and cook 5 minutes.
2. Toss in the garlic and cook 30 seconds.
3. Insert the tomatoes and stir to coat with oil. Place aside to cool. Transfer the tomatoes in Sous Vide bag.
4. Add the remaining ingredients and seal using water immersion technique. Cook the tomatoes 50 minutes.
5. Remove the bag from the cooker. Open the bag and chill 15 minutes. Peel the tomatoes and place in a food blender, with cooking juices.

6. Discard the herbs. Blend the tomatoes until smooth. Serve or use later.

Cook's Tip: This incredibly delicious song goes perfectly with pasta.

Serves: 12   **Prep Time:** 10mins   **Cook Time:** 50mins
Calories: 42   **Protein:** 1g   **Carbs:** 4.9g   **Fat:** 2.5g

Cranberry Sauce

Ingredients:
- 3 cups cranberries
- ½ cup sugar
- ½ orange, zested

Directions:
1. Preheat Sous Vide cooker to 180F. Combine all ingredients in a Sous Vide bag.
2. Vacuum seal the bag and cook the cranberries 2 hours.
3. Remove the bag from the cooker. Leave the cranberries to cool completely in a bag.
4. Once cooled, transfer to a serving bowl.

Cook's Tip: Pair this delicious sauce with your Thanksgiving turkey to seal in a lot more flavor on your holiday plate.

Serves: 6   **Prep Time: 10mins**   **Cook Time: 2 hrs.**
Calories: 100   **Protein: 0.1g**   **Carbs: 23.5g**   **Fat: 0g**

Hot Sauce

Ingredients:
- 1 ½ lb. jalapenos, seeded and chopped
- 1/3 cup rice wine vinegar
- 6 cloves garlic, minced
- 3 tablespoons light honey
- 1 teaspoon fine salt

Directions:
1. Preheat Sous Vide cooker to 210F. Combine jalapenos, garlic, and salt into Sous vide bag.
2. Seal the bag using water immersion technique.
3. Submerge the bag into a water bath and cook 25 minutes.
4. Remove the bag from the water bath and pour the content into a bowl. Stir in the vinegar and honey. Serve or store in a fridge.

Cook's Tip: This spicy treat goes great with steak and other red meats.

Serves: 10　　**Prep Time: 5mins**　　**Cook Time: 25mins**
Calories: 28　　**Protein: 1g**　　**Carbs: 4.6g**　　**Fat: 0.4g**

Applesauce

Ingredients:
- 3 apples, coarsely chopped
- 1 cinnamon stick

Directions:
1. Preheat the water bath to 170°F.
2. Seal all ingredients in the bag. Cook 3 hours.
3. Transfer apples to a bowl. Remove cinnamon stick.
4. Mash to your desired consistency.

Cook's Tip: This spicy treat goes great with steak and other red meats.

Serves: 2 **Prep Time:** 30mins **Cook Time:** 3hrs
Calories: 142 **Protein:** 0.7g **Carbs:** 37.7g **Fat:** 0.46g

Sweet and Sour Sauce

Ingredients:
- 1/3 cup olive oil
- 1 shallot, chopped
- 1 cup fresh pineapple chunks
- ¼ cup rice vinegar
- Salt and pepper, to taste

Directions:
1. Preheat Sous Vide cooker to 130F. Combine all ingredients in a Sous Vide bag.
2. Seal the bag using immersion water technique. Cook the pineapple 2 hours.
3. Remove the bag from the cooker.
4. Open the bag and allow to cool 10 minutes.
5. Transfer the pineapple, and cooking juices into a food blender. Blend until smooth. Serve.

Cook's Tip: This delicious sauce pairs well with most American-Asian fusion dishes like Sweet and Sour chicken or shrimp.

Serves: 6　　　　**Prep Time: 10mins**　　**Cook Time: 2 hrs.**
Calories: 118　　**Protein: 0.2g**　　　　**Carbs: 3.9g**　　**Fat: 11.2g**

Basil Tomato Sauce

Ingredients:
- 1 can (28-ounce) whole tomatoes, crushed
- 1 onion, diced
- 2 cloves garlic, minced
- 1 tablespoon olive oil
- 1 bay leaf
- 1 sprig rosemary
- ½ teaspoon salt
- ½ teaspoon pepper
- 1 cup fresh basil, chopped
- Cooked pasta for serving

Directions:
1. Preheat the water bath to 185°F.
2. Combine all ingredients in a bag. Seal and place in water bath. Cook 1 hour.
3. Remove bay leaves and rosemary sprig. Serve with cooked pasta.

Cook's Tip: The basil in this recipe adds an extra kick to the traditional tomato sauce. Try using this in place of ketchup for an elevated French fry dip or to create an homemade pizza.

Serves: 2　　　　　**Prep Time:** 20mins　　　**Cook Time:** 1 hr.
Calories: 158　　　**Protein:** 4.57g　　　　**Carbs:** 21.4g　　**Fat:** 7.9.g

Creme Anglaise

Ingredients:
- 3 egg yolks
- ½ cup milk
- ¼ cup heavy cream
- ¼ cup sugar
- 1 teaspoon vanilla

Directions:
1. Preheat the water bath to 170°F.
2. Combine all ingredients in a bag. Seal and cook 20 minutes.
3. Blend sauce until smooth. Transfer to refrigerator and cool completely before serving.

Cook's Tip: This sauce pairs brilliantly with sweet applications such as cakes or poached fruits.

Serves: 2 **Prep Time:** 20mins **Cook Time:** 20mins
Calories: 277 **Protein:** 6.58g **Carbs:** 17.4g **Fat:** 19.7g

Soy Chili Sauce

Ingredients:
- 1 cup light soy sauce
- 2 green chilies, chopped, seeded
- ¼ cup honey
- 1 teaspoon cumin

Directions:
1. Preheat Sous Vide cooker to 160F. Combine all ingredients in Sous Vide bag.
2. Seal using water immersion technique. Submerge the bag into the water bath.
3. Cook 30 minutes.
4. Remove the bag from cooker and serve sauce in a bowl.

Cook's Tip: This sauce pairs brilliantly with summer spring rolls made with rice paper.

Serves: 8 **Prep Time: 5mins** **Cook Time: 30mins**
Calories: 35 **Protein: 0.5g** **Carbs: 10.8g** **Fat: 0.1g**

Cherry Sauce

Ingredients:
- 3 cups cherries
- ½ cup sugar
- ½ lemon, zested

Directions:
1. Preheat Sous Vide cooker to 180F. Combine all ingredients in a Sous Vide bag.
2. Vacuum seal the bag and cook the cherries 2 hours.
3. Remove the bag from the cooker. Leave the cherries to cool completely in a bag.
4. Once cooled, transfer to a serving bowl.

Cook's Tip: This sauce pairs brilliantly with summer spring rolls made with rice paper.

Serves: 6   **Prep Time: 10mins**   **Cook Time: 2 hrs.**
Calories: 100   **Protein: 0.1g**   **Carbs: 23.5g**   **Fat: 0g**

Chapter 10: Sous Vide Cocktail & Dessert Recipes

Orange-Anise Bitters

Ingredients:
- The peel of one orange, pit removed
- 1 star anise
- 1 cup bourbon

Directions:
1. Preheat the water bath to 125°F. Seal all ingredients in a bag and place in water bath.
2. Cook 2 hours. Strain bitters into a small bottle using a coffee filter or a cheesecloth.
3. Before using a cocktail strainer, bring to room temperature.

Cook's Tip: Consider adding the peels of both bitter and sweet oranges for a more intense flavor.

Serves: 4	**Prep Time: 10mins**	**Cook Time: 2 hrs**
Calories: 140	**Protein: 0.3g**	**Carbs: 0.06g Fat: 0.2g**

Lime-Ginger Gin Tonic

Ingredients:
- 1 cup gin
- 1 lime, cut into wedges
- 1-inch ginger, peeled
- 1 ¼ cup tonic water
- 1 cup ice

Directions:
1. Preheat the water bath to 125°F.
2. Pour gin, ginger, and half the lime into a bag. Seal and place in water bath. Cook 2 hours. After 2 hours, remove to the refrigerator and cool completely.
3. When gin infusion is cool, divide ice between 4 glasses. Strain solids from the gin.
4. Pour an equal amount of the gin infusion into each glass. Garnish with lime wedge.

Cook's Tip: If you are unable to find tonic water while creating the drink, sparkling water is just as good.

Serves: 4   **Prep Time: 20mins**   **Cook Time: 2 hrs.**
Calories: 630   **Protein: 0.22g**   **Carbs: 30.9g**   **Fat: 0.05g**

Mocha Coffee Liqueur

Ingredients:
- 1 ½ cups vodka
- 1 lb. coffee beans
- ½ cup cacao nibs
- 1 cup sugar
- 1 vanilla bean, split

Directions:
1. Preheat sous vide to 150°F.
2. Combine all ingredients in a bag and seal. Place in water bath and cook 24 hours.
3. Strain solids from the bag using a coffee filter or cheesecloth.
4. Transfer to a bottle and bring to room temperature before using in your favorite cocktails.

Cook's Tip: To give this an even fuller taste add a bit of espresso to the mixture before sealing.

Serves: 8 **Prep Time: 20mins** **Cook Time: 24 hrs.**
Calories: 244 **Protein: 1.7g** **Carbs: 21.49g** **Fat: 6.3g**

Strawberry Ice Cream

Ingredients:
- 2 cups strawberries
- ½ cup fine sugar
- 1 cup heavy cream
- 1 cup milk
- 5 egg yolks
- ½ cup granulated sugar
- 1 teaspoon vanilla paste

Directions:
1. Set the sous vide cooker to preheat to 180 degrees F. Add sugar and strawberries to a vacuum pack bag. Seal, and set to cook in the bath for about 30 minutes.
2. Remove the bag from the cooker and strain the strawberries through the fine mesh sieve, pressing to remove pulp. Discard the seeds.
3. Combine heavy cream, milk, egg yolks, granulated sugar, and vanilla paste in a food blender.
4. Blend until smooth. Stir in the strawberry mixture and transfer all into a large bag.

5. Seal the bag using water immersion technique and cook in Sous Vide cooker for 1 hour.
6. When the timer goes off, remove the bag from the cooker and lace into ice-cold water bath 30 minutes.
7. Churn the mixture into an ice cream machine until set. Serve.

Cook's Tip: This delicious ice cream and be served on top of cookies or brownies as a treat for the kids or young at heart.

Serves: 6   **Prep Time: 30mins**   **Cook Time: 1 hr 30min**
Calories: 218   **Protein: 4.5g**   **Carbs: 24.6g**   **Fat: 12.3g**

Peach Infused Bourbon

Ingredients:
- 2 ripe peaches, cut into wedges, pit and peel removed
- 1 cinnamon stick
- 2 cups bourbon

Directions:
1. Preheat the water bath to 150°F. Seal all ingredients in a bag. Place in water bath and cook 2 hours.
2. Strain solids from brandy using a cheesecloth or coffee filter.
3. Bring to room temperature before using in cocktails

Cook's Tip: This drink is best served with steak or red meat.

Serves: 8 **Prep Time: 20mins** **Cook Time: 2 hrs.**
Calories: 143 **Protein: 0.3g** **Carbs: 3.58g** **Fat: 0.1g**

"Barrel-Aged" Negroni

Ingredients:
- ½ cup gin
- ½ cup vermouth
- ½ cup Campari
- ½ cup water
- 1 orange, cut into wedges
- ½ cup winemaking toasted oak chips

Directions:
1. Preheat the water bath to 120°F.
2. Combine all ingredients in a bag. Seal and place in water bath. Cook 24 hours.
3. Strain solids from liquid using a coffee filter or cheesecloth. Serve over ice.

Cook's Tip: If you are short on Gin you can swap it out for whiskey for a similar effect.

Serves: 4 **Prep Time: 20mins** **Cook Time: 20mins**
Calories: 216 **Protein: 0.07g** **Carbs: 17.3g Fat: 0.07g**

Tom Collins Cocktail

Ingredients:
- 7 cups gin
- 1 cup lemon juice
- 2 cups lemon rind
- 1 ½ cups granulated sugar
- Soda water, to serve with

Directions:
1. Preheat Sous Vide to 131F. In a large Sous vide bag, combine gin, lemon juice, lemon rind, and sugar. Fold the edges of the bag few times and clip to the side of your pot. Cook the cocktail 1 hour.
2. Strain the cocktail into a large glass jug. Place aside to cool completely before use.
3. Serve over ice and finish off with soda water.

Cook's Tip: This delicious drink can be garnished with lemon rind or fresh thyme.

Serves: 20　**Prep Time:** 10mins　**Cook Time:** 1 hr
Calories: 270　**Protein:** 0.3g　**Carbs:** 17.2g　**Fat:** 0.2g

Cherry Manhattan

Ingredients:
Bourbon infusion:
- 2 cups bourbon
- ¼ cup raw cacao nibs
- 1 cup dried cherries

To finish:
- 4oz. sweet vermouth
- 1 Chocolate bitters, as desired

Directions:
1. Make the infusion; preheat Sous Vide to 122F. In a Sous Vide bag combine bourbon, cacao nibs, and cherries. Seal the bag, and cook 1 hour
2. Remove the bag from the water bath and let cool. Strain the content into a jar.
3. Fill the tall glasses with ice. Add chocolate bitters (3 dashes per serving) and 1/8 of the infused bourbon. Skewer the Sous vide cherries and garnish.

Cook's Tip: Swap the cocoa nibs for coffee beans to create a stronger drink.

Serves: 8 **Prep Time:** 10mins **Cook Time:** 1 hr.
Calories: 163 **Protein:** 0.4g **Carbs:** 2.2g **Fat:** 1.3g

Rummy Eggnog

Ingredients:
- 4 eggs
- 2 cups whole milk
- 1 cup heavy cream
- ½ tablespoon vanilla
- ¾ cup sugar
- 2 cinnamon sticks
- ½ cup rum
- Freshly-grated nutmeg for garnish

Directions:
1. Preheat the water bath to 140°F. Beat eggs until pale and fluffy. Beat in milk, cream, vanilla, and sugar.
2. Pour into bag with the cinnamon stick and seal using water immersion method. Place bag in water bath and cook 1 hour.
3. Strain solids from the bag using a coffee filter or cheesecloth. Chill completely.
4. To serve, pour into glasses and top with freshly-grated nutmeg.

Cook's Tip: The rum can be omitted for a non – alcoholic treat. In this case consider adding in a bit more cream to suffice.

Serves: 4 **Prep Time:** 30mins **Cook Time:** 1 hr.
Calories: 551 **Protein:** 14g **Carbs:** 27.4g **Fat:** 35.54g

Watermelon Mint Vodka Infusion

Ingredients:
- 1 cup vodka
- 1 cup watermelon, cubed
- 2-3 sprigs fresh mint

Directions:
1. Preheat the water bath to 140°F. Seal all ingredients in a bag.
2. Place in water bath and cook 2 hours.
3. Strain solids from the infusion. Use in your favorite martini recipe.

Cook's Tip: This infusion can be used in martini's, Jell-O shots and so much more.

Serves: 4 **Prep Time:** 20mins **Cook Time:** 2 hrs.
Calories: 140 **Protein:** 0.1g **Carbs:** 17.2g **Fat:** 0.2g

Bloody Mary Cocktail

Ingredients:
- 6 tomatoes, quartered
- ¼ cup horseradish (from a jar)
- ¼ cup Worcestershire sauce
- 2 cups vodka
- 1 jalapeno pepper, halved, seeded
- ½ cup lime juice

To serve with:
- Salt, Celery Stalks

Directions:
1. Heat Sous Vide cooker to 145F. In a Sous Vide bag, combine all ingredients.
2. Seal the bag and set to cook for about 3 hours.
3. Remove the bag from the water bath. Strain through a fine-mesh sieve and press the tomatoes to release any remaining pulp.
4. Allow cooling completely before serving. Make a salt rim around the glass.

5. Serve the Bloody Mary in a glass along with a celery stalk.

Cook's Tip: This drink pairs well with cheesy foods like mozzarella sticks or nachos.

Serves: 8 **Prep Time: 10mins** **Cook Time: 3 hrs**
Calories: 150 **Protein: 0.9g** **Carbs: 6.3g** **Fat: 0.2g**

Conclusion

You did it! Congrats on getting all the way to the end of our 101 Seasonal Recipes for the Sous Vide Cooker: Over 100 Easy & Delicious Sous Vide Recipes! This was indeed your very first hurdle to becoming a Master of Sous Vide, and the first of many positive hurdles to come.

I hope you have enjoyed all 101 delicious Sous Vide recipes, and that you will continue to enjoy them with your whole family and friends.

What happens next?

The next step is to continue practicing and enjoying the recipes as you see fit. Then when you are ready to begin another adventure join us again on yet another one of our amazing culinary journeys. Remember to leave us a positive review if you liked what you read.

If you'd like more FREE recipes…

[You can head over here to claim it for FREE.](http://inspiyration.com/healthy) (http://inspiyration.com/healthy)

Also, stay updated by signing up to my newsletter for awesome cooking tips, mouth-watering recipes, and more…

See you inside!

Until next time, keep on cooking. Best of luck :)

Index

2

279 Protein: 8.9g Carbs: 3.4g Fat: 25.6g, **96**

A

acorn squash, **74**
Acorn Squash, **74**
all-purpose flour, **26**, **27**, **40**
almond milk, **110**
almonds, **26**, **27**
anchovy, **85**
apple juice, **148**
apples, **79**, **166**
Apples, **79**
Applesauce, **166**
Aromatic Chicken, 63
Artichokes, **99**
asparagus, **93**, **103**, **104**
Asparagus, **93**, **103**
Asparagus with Hollandaise, **93**
Autumn, 74
avocado, **56**, **57**

B

baby back ribs, **38**
bacon, **28**, **54**, **55**, **60**, **75**, **81**, **153**
Bacon, **28**, **75**
bacon,, **60**, **75**, **81**
barbecue sauce, **152**
basil, **32**, **33**, **62**, **63**, **65**, **125**, **162**, **169**
Basil, **169**
Basil Tomato Sauce, **169**
bay leaf, **46**, **47**, **148**, **169**
bay leaves, **52**, **53**, **72**, **155**, **169**
BBQ sauce, **38**, **39**
beef, **36**, **37**, **40**, **41**, **44**, **48**, **50**, **51**, **52**, **53**, **54**, **55**
Beef, **36**, **40**, **50**, **54**
beef brisket, **36**
Beef Brisket, **36**
beef loin, **40**

beef stock, **36**, **40**, **41**, **52**, **53**
Beef Stroganoff, **40**
beef tenderloin, **50**
Beef Wellington, **50**
Beet, **87**
Beet Salad, **87**
beets, **87**
Beets, **87**
bell peppers, **70**
Bloody Mary, **187**, **188**
BLT, **153**
bourbon, **174**, **180**, **183**
Bourbon, **180**, **183**
bread, **52**, **101**, **102**, **130**, **153**, **155**
breadcrumbs, **130**
brisket, **36**, **37**
Brisket, **36**
broccoli, **85**, **104**
Broccoli, **85**
Broccoli Salad, **85**
broccolini, **67**
Broccolini, **67**
brown sugar, **38**, **79**, **112**, **146**, **148**, **152**
Brussels, **75**, **109**
Brussels sprouts, **75**, **109**
Brussels Sprouts, **75**, **109**
Burger Buns, **44**
Burgers, **44**
butter, **18**, **22**, **26**, **27**, **32**, **34**, **40**, **41**, **50**, **51**, **52**, **53**, **58**, **67**, **70**, **71**, **74**, **75**, **83**, **89**, **91**, **94**, **96**, **99**, **106**, **108**, **113**, **127**, **132**, **133**, **160**, **161**
Butter, **94**, **96**, **99**, **103**, **118**
Buttercup Squash, **112**
buttermilk, **125**

C

cabbage, **87**, **88**, **114**
cacao nibs, **177**, **183**
Cajun spice, **127**
Campari, **181**
capers, **32**, **33**, **121**, **122**
caraway, **101**

Carnitas, **72**
Carnitas Tacos, **72**
carrot, **155**
carrots, **36**, **37**, **54**, **87**, **140**, **156**
Carrots, **87**
cauliflower, **85**, **91**, **101**, **102**, **106**
Cauliflower, **91**, **101**, **106**
Cauliflower Puree, **91**
Cauliflower Soup, **101**
celery, **136**, **137**, **140**, **155**, **156**, **188**
Celery Stalks, **187**
cheese, **58**, **62**
Cheese, **44**
cherries, **173**, **183**
Cherry, **173**, **183**
Cherry Sauce, **173**
cherry tomatoes, **85**
chicken, **60**, **63**, **64**, **65**, **70**, **71**, **81**, **83**, **84**, **106**, **123**, **125**, **130**, **134**, **135**, **136**, **137**, **138**, **140**, **141**, **146**
Chicken, 63, 65, 70, 83, 123, 125, 130, 134, 136, 138, 140
chicken breast, **65**, **136**, **138**
chicken breasts, **63**, **65**, **83**, **130**, **134**, **137**
Chicken Cordon Bleu, **130**
chicken drums, **125**
Chicken Salad, **136**
Chicken Soup, **140**
chicken stock, **60**, **63**, **81**, **83**, **106**
Chicken Teriyaki, **134**
chicken thighs, **70**, **71**
Chicken Thighs, **70**
chicken wings, **123**
Chicken Wings, **123**
chili, **26**, **30**, **31**, **58**, **63**, **97**, **138**, **157**
chili peppers, **30**
chili powder, **26**, **58**
chili sauce, **63**
chilies, **172**
chives, **70**, **136**, **137**
Chives, **94**
Chocolate bitters, **183**
chuck, **48**
cider, **60**
cider vinegar, **60**, **81**, **148**
cilantro, **58**, **72**, **73**, **96**, **141**
Cilantro, **96**, **140**
cinnamon, **157**, **166**, **180**, **184**

cinnamon sticks, **184**
circulator, **11**, **12**, **15**
cocoa powder, **157**
coconut oil, **140**
coffee, **174**, **177**, **180**, **181**, **184**
coffee beans, **177**
Cooking Temperatures, **9**
Cordial, **112**
coriander, **30**, **31**, **38**, **140**
Coriander, **30**
corn, **58**
Corn, **58**, **72**, **96**
Corn tortillas, **72**
Cotija, **58**
Cotija cheese, **58**
crab, **56**, **57**
Crab, **56**
crab legs, **56**
cranberries, **164**
Cranberry, **164**
Cranberry Sauce, **164**
cream, **35**, **87**, **101**, **102**, **114**, **116**, **171**, **178**, **179**, **184**
Creme Anglaise, **171**
crème Fraiche, **40**, **41**, **56**, **57**
crushed red pepper, **123**, **140**, **141**
cumin, **38**, **42**, **72**, **101**, **102**, **116**, **117**, **150**, **157**, **172**
Cumin, **42**
curry powder, **74**, **140**

D

Delicata Squash, **113**
Dijon mustard, **54**, **142**
dill, **24**, **87**, **88**, **114**
DIY Method, **12**
DIY vacuum sealer, **13**
Duck, **127**, **132**
duck breast, **132**
duck wings, **127**
Duck Wings, **127**

E

egg, **20**, **21**, **44**, **50**, **51**, **111**, **130**, **144**, **160**, **161**, **171**, **178**
Egg Muffins, **110**
egg noodles, **20**, **21**

egg yolks, **160**, **161**, **171**, **178**
Eggnog, **184**
eggs, **94**, **110**, **184**
Eggs, **9**, **94**
Essential Cooking Equipment:, **13**
extra virgin olive oil, **85**

F

Fall, **74**
fennel, **119**, **120**
Fennel, **119**
feta, **62**
Feta, **62**
feta cheese, **62**
fish, **17**, **22**, **27**, **28**, **104**, **138**, **140**
Fish, **9**, **18**, **26**, **28**
fish sauce, **104**, **138**, **140**
flour, **26**, **27**, **41**, **52**, **53**, **83**, **125**, **130**

G

Gala apples, **79**
garam masala, **74**
garlic, **22**, **30**, **31**, **32**, **33**, **34**, **36**, **37**, **38**, **42**, **46**, **47**, **52**, **53**, **63**, **67**, **68**, **72**, **75**, **77**, **83**, **97**, **99**, **106**, **109**, **121**, **122**, **125**, **129**, **132**, **136**, **137**, **138**, **140**, **144**, **148**, **152**, **155**, **156**, **157**, **162**, **165**, **169**
Garlic, **30**, **67**, **80**, **99**
Garlic Confit, **80**
Garlic Parmesan Broccolini, **67**
Garlic Squids, **30**
gin, **175**, **181**, **182**
Gin, **175**
ginger, **20**, **21**, **30**, **31**, **77**, **97**, **134**, **175**
Ginger, **97**, **175**
ginger juice, **134**
granulated sugar, **178**
Greek yogurt, **24**, **94**
green beans, **104**
ground almonds, **26**

H

ham, **130**
heavy cream, **34**, **171**
Herbed Rice, **70**
Hollandaise, **93**, **161**

honey, **36**, **37**, **127**, **159**, **165**, **172**
Honey, **159**
horseradish, **187**
hot sauce, **127**
Hot Sauce, **165**

I

Immersion Circulator, **15**
Immersion Circulator:, **11**
Indian, **77**

J

jalapeno, **187**
jalapenos, **165**

K

ketchup, **127**, **142**, **159**

L

lamb, **42**, **46**, **47**
Lamb, **36**, **42**, **46**
Lamb Chops, **42**
lamb shanks, **46**
Lamb Shanks, **46**
Leek, **110**, **114**
leeks, **110**, **114**
lemon, **22**, **24**, **26**, **28**, **30**, **31**, **32**, **33**, **46**, **47**, **63**, **64**, **99**, **101**, **102**, **116**, **117**, **121**, **129**, **136**, **137**, **173**, **182**
Lemon, **99**, **121**
lemon juice, **26**, **28**, **32**, **33**, **47**
Lemon zest, **99**
lettuce, **20**, **21**, **137**, **153**
lime, **18**, **56**, **58**, **73**, **140**, **141**, **175**, **187**
Lime, **58**, **72**, **175**
lime juice, **56**
lime zest, **58**
lobster, **18**, **34**
Lobster, **18**, **34**
lobster tail, **18**
long grain rice, **70**

M

Manhattan, **183**

maple, **79**, **142**, **159**
maple whiskey, **79**
marsala wine, **83**
Mason Jars, **15**
mayonnaise, **58**, **136**, **137**, **153**
Mediterranean Chicken, **65**
Mexican, **58**
milk, **106**, **110**, **171**, **178**, **184**
mint, **46**, **47**, **186**
Mint, **103**, **186**
mirin, **97**
Miso, **118**
Miso-Butter, **118**
Mocha Coffee, **177**
Mocha Coffee Liqueur, **177**
Mousse, **56**
mushrooms, **40**, **41**, **50**, **51**
mushrooms,, **50**, **83**
mustard, **55**, **68**, **119**, **127**, **136**, **137**, **142**, **148**, **159**
Mustard, **159**
mustard powder, **68**

N

Negroni, **181**
Nonstick Pan and Cast-iron Skillet, **15**
noodles, **40**, **41**
nutmeg, **184**

O

olive oil, **28**, **30**, **31**, **32**, **36**, **37**, **42**, **48**, **52**, **53**, **56**, **57**, **63**, **65**, **70**, **71**, **78**, **85**, **101**, **110**, **116**, **120**, **121**, **122**, **144**, **150**, **155**, **156**, **157**, **162**, **167**, **169**
Olive oil, **80**, **119**
Omelet, **94**
onion, **21**, **60**, **72**, **81**, **83**, **87**, **114**, **125**, **136**, **140**, **141**, **144**, **152**, **155**, **156**, **157**, **158**, **169**
Onion, **44**
Onion rings, **44**
orange, **120**, **132**, **164**, **174**, **181**
Orange, **132**, **174**
Orange-Anise, **174**
oregano, **46**, **47**, **91**, **162**
Osso Bucco, **155**

P

paprika, **36**, **37**, **38**, **68**, **70**, **71**, **152**
Parmesan, **67**
parsley, **38**, **44**, **68**, **70**, **108**, **119**, **120**, **136**, **137**, **144**, **150**, **162**
Parsley, **94**
parsnips, **89**
pasta, **21**, **83**, **169**
Peach, **180**
peaches, **180**
peas, **54**
peppers, **47**, **70**, **71**
Piccata, **32**
pineapple, **157**, **158**, **167**
Plastic Bags, **14**
poblano pepper, **157**
polenta, **46**, **47**
pork, **72**, **73**, **77**, **78**, **142**, **144**, **146**, **147**, **148**, **150**, **152**, **155**, **157**, **159**
Pork, **77**, **142**, **146**, **148**, **150**, **155**, **157**, **159**
pork belly, **146**
Pork Knuckles, **148**
Pork Loin, **157**
Pork Medallions, **150**
pork ribs, **152**
pork shoulder, **72**, **142**, **159**
Pork Shoulder, **159**
Potato, **60**
Potato Salad, **60**
potato,, **87**, **89**, **116**
potatoes, **60**, **61**
prosciutto, **50**, **51**
Provençale, **52**
puff pastry, **50**, **51**
pumpkin, **89**
Pumpkin, **89**
Pumpkin Puree, **89**

R

Radish, **62**
Radish Feta Salad, **62**
radishes, **62**
ramen, **146**, **147**
Ramen, **146**
ramen noodles, **146**, **147**
Ras el Hanout, **101**, **102**
red curry paste, **140**

red onion, **20**
red peppers, **46**
red snapper, **22**
Red Snapper, **22**
red wine, **36**
ribs, **38**, **39**, **52**, **53**
Ribs, **38**, **52**, **152**
rice, **13**, **23**, **70**, **71**, **165**, **167**
Rice, **70**
rice wine vinegar, **165**
Roast, **37**, **48**
Rolled Beef, **54**
rosemary, **22**, **46**, **47**, **48**, **52**, **53**, **121**, **144**, **155**, **169**
Rosemary, **94**, **121**
Roulade, **56**
rum, **184**

S

Safety, **17**
sage, **89**, **91**, **113**, **129**, **144**
sake, **134**, **135**
Salad, **44**, **62**, **81**, **85**, **87**, **104**, **114**, **119**, **136**
salmon, **20**, **21**, **24**, **25**, **110**, **121**, **122**
Salmon, **20**, **24**, **110**, **121**
sandwich bags, **14**
Saucepan, **16**
scallions, **20**, **21**, **60**, **61**, **81**, **82**, **104**, **140**, **141**, **146**
Seafood, **18**
Sesame, **104**
sesame dressing, **20**, **21**
sesame oil, **20**, **21**, **104**
sesame seeds, **20**, **21**, **104**
shallot, **50**, **68**, **83**, **102**, **116**, **132**, **160**, **167**
shallots, **40**, **41**, **51**, **101**, **102**, **116**, **140**, **141**
sherry, **34**, **132**, **133**, **146**
sherry vinegar, **132**, **133**
Short Ribs, **52**
Sicilian Lamb, **46**
smoked paprika, **36**
snapper, **22**
sole, **28**
Sole, **28**
Sole Fish, **28**
sour cream, **77**, **88**, **101**, **102**, **114**, **116**
Sour cream,, **87**, **114**
Sous Vide Machines, **10**

Soy Chili Sauce, **172**
soy sauce, **20**, **21**, **97**, **104**, **127**, **134**, **135**, **142**, **146**, **159**, **172**
Spiced Ribs, **38**
spinach, **62**, **140**, **141**
squash, **74**, **112**, **113**
Squash, **74**, **112**, **113**
squids, **30**, **31**
Squids, **30**
star anise, **174**
stock, **37**, **60**, **83**, **87**, **88**, **102**, **114**, **116**
strawberries, **178**
Strawberry, **178**
Stroganoff, **40**
sugar, **54**, **62**, **79**, **97**, **108**, **119**, **134**, **135**, **138**, **140**, **146**, **152**, **164**, **171**, **173**, **177**, **178**, **182**, **184**
Summer, **56**
Summer Recipes, **56**
sun-dried tomatoes, **65**
Sweet and Sour Sauce, **167**
sweet potato, **89**, **116**
Sweet Potato, **81**, **116**
sweet potatoes, **81**
Swiss cheese, **130**
swordfish, **32**
Swordfish, **32**

T

Tacos, **72**
tarragon, **18**, **136**, **137**, **160**
Tarragon, **94**
tenderloin, **50**
Teriyaki, **20**, **134**
teriyaki sauce, **20**, **21**
thyme, **34**, **36**, **37**, **40**, **41**, **52**, **53**, **54**, **70**, **71**, **123**, **132**, **144**, **148**, **155**
tofu, **97**
Tofu, **97**
Tom Collins, **182**
tomato, **36**, **37**, **46**, **47**, **50**, **51**, **52**, **53**, **153**
Tomato, **162**, **169**
tomato paste, **36**, **37**, **46**, **47**, **50**, **51**, **52**, **53**
tomatoes, **65**, **68**, **85**, **155**, **156**, **162**, **163**, **169**, **187**
Tomatoes, **44**
tonic water, **175**
tuna, **26**, **27**

Tuna, **26**
turkey, **68, 129**
Turkey, **68, 129**
Turkey Burgers, **68**
turmeric, **140**
turnips, **108, 118**
Turnips, **108, 118**

V

Vacuum Sealer, **14**
Vacuum Sealer:, **14**
vanilla, **171, 177, 178, 184**
vanilla bean, **177**
vegetable oil, **26, 30, 31, 54, 70, 71, 104, 123, 130**
vegetable stock, **101, 116**
vermouth, **181, 183**
vinegar, **60, 62, 81, 87, 88, 114, 119, 165, 167**
vodka, **112, 177, 186, 187**
Vodka, **186**

W

Water Basin, **15**
watermelon, **186**
Watermelon, **186**
whiskey, **79**
Whiskey, **79**
White asparagus, **103**
white wine, **62**
white wine vinegar, **119, 161**
wine, **36, 37, 40, 41, 52, 53, 62, 83, 87, 101, 102, 114, 116, 119, 132, 133, 155, 156, 160, 161, 165**
Worcestershire sauce, **56, 187**

Y

yellow mustard, **119**
Yogurt Dill Sauce, **24**
Yukon Gold Potato, **60**
Yukon Gold potatoes, **60**

Z

zest, **58**
Ziploc bag, **13**
Ziploc freezer bag, **13**
zucchini, **56, 57**
Zucchini, **56**
Zucchini Roulade, **56**

Made in the USA
San Bernardino, CA
08 June 2018